The Golden Avant-Garde

Cultural Frames, Framing Culture

ROBERT NEWMAN, *Editor*

The Golden Avant-Garde

Idolatry, Commercialism, and Art

Raphael Sassower and
Louis Cicotello

UNIVERSITY PRESS OF VIRGINIA

◇ Charlottesville and London

The University Press of Virginia

© 2000 by the Rector and Visitors of the University of Virginia

All rights reserved

Printed in the United States of America

First published in 2000

⊗ The paper used in this publication meets the minimum requirements of the American National Standard for Information Sciences—Permanence of Paper for Printed Library Materials, ANSI Z39.48-1984.

Library of Congress Cataloging-in-Publication Data

Sassower, Raphael.
    The golden avant-garde: idolatry, commercialism, and art / Raphael Sassower and Louis Cicotello.
       p. cm.—(Cultural frames, framing culture)
    Includes bibliographical references and index.
    ISBN 0-8139-1934-7 (cloth: alk. paper)—ISBN 0-8139-1935-5 (paper: alk. paper)
    1. Art and society—History—20th century. 2. Avant-garde (Aesthetics)—History—20th century. I. Cicotello, Louis, 1940– II. Title. III. Series.

N72.S6 S29 2000
701'.03—dc21   99-055194

Dedicated to the memory of

Louis J. and Katherine A. Cicotello

and

Marx Wartofsky

Contents

Acknowledgments

We would like to thank two insightful reviewers, Ellen Willis and Robert Newman, whose careful reading and critical and supportive commentary helped sharpen our presentation. Our home institution stayed out of our intellectual way, and that, too, is worthy of gratitude in the current climate of the academy. Finally, we wish to thank our students whose endurance during a team-taught seminar on aesthetics suggested to us that this book may be read by a wider audience than we originally expected.

The Golden Avant-Garde

Introduction

And it was said to the artisans: Heed your skill and fashion
works that will forever be our riches and your glory!

—Cicotello and Sassower, with apologies to the Bible

THE FABRICATION of golden calves has been an ongoing enterprise
under different guises and with many different intentions. Let us
recall the original tale:

> And when the people saw that Moses delayed to come down
> from the mount, the people gathered themselves together unto
> Aaron, and said unto him: "Up, make us a god who shall go
> before us; for as for this Moses, the man that brought us up out
> of the land of Egypt, we know not what has become of him."
> And Aaron said unto them: "Break off the golden rings,
> which are in the ears of your wives, of your sons, and of your
> daughters, and bring them unto me."
> And all the people broke off the golden rings which were in
> their ears, and brought them unto Aaron.
> And he received it at their hand, and fashioned it with a grav-
> ing tool, and made it a molten calf; and they said: "This is thy
> god, O Israel, which brought thee up out of the land of Egypt."
> And when Aaron saw this, he built an altar before it; and
> Aaron made proclamation, and said: "Tomorrow shall be a feast
> to the LORD."
> And they rose up early on the morrow, and offered burnt-
> offerings, and brought peace-offerings; and the people sat down
> to eat and drink, and rose up to make merry. (Exod. 32:1–6)

Exodus records the inherent and greater appeal of a molten gold calf
(considered a bull-calf in most translations) in comparison to the appeal

2 of an invisible God who uses a stutterer such as Moses as his messenger.
◇ This story is told as a warning against the tendency to stray from God's commandments and follow idols or icons shimmering in the sunlight and encouraging feasts or orgies to satisfy human desires. The discipline of monotheism seems a hardship in light of the immediacy of sensual experiences and the gratification that material possessions bring about. This passage from Exodus implores humanity to retain its spiritual and moral high ground.

The culture of idolatry remains intact despite two thousand years of monotheism. That is, desire and aesthetic gratification cannot be overcome by scripture and custom. Human desire and the pleasure principle, as Freud so eloquently argued, retain their vitality and potential for explosion. Artists can sit back and draw scenes of the worship of the golden calf (for example, Emil Nolde's 1910 work *Dance around the Golden Calf,* where garish exaggerations reflect a condemnation), or they can be the ones fabricating it for a fee; they even can do both. The precious gold earrings are willingly traded for a sculpture, an idol, a god worth worshipping. And artists are there to accommodate the needs of their patrons, to further the goals of their leaders (in the ancient case, Aaron). Should they refuse the commission? Should they not participate in their culture's upheaval? Can they refrain from taking part in their own culture? More important for our purposes, to what extent are they conscious of this condition and other, related predicaments? These complex questions form the core of our investigations into the role of the avant-garde in contemporary culture.

Artists perform a useful task for their culture, constructing national and religious monuments that express and honor their most valuable principles and goals, and society has learned to rely on them for this task. It would be odd to see artists do otherwise than complete that for which they get rewarded. But society since the eighteenth century has also fabricated a fascinating myth about artists as revolutionary heroes who defy the authorities and pay dearly for their passion and vision. The predicament wherein artists have found themselves over the past centuries parallels that of scientists (as argued elsewhere, Sassower) in the sense that they face expectations that they cannot meet under the conditions set for them by the public. The main difference is that the history of the artists' predicament dates to earlier times.

What fascinates us is the extent to which artists in general, and avant-garde artists in particular (as conventionally defined in art-critical discourse), have been able to cope with this predicament over the past century. They are still called upon to fabricate golden calves to rescue a culture from its confusion and anxiety, and yet they know that the wrath of God and king is always simmering in the background, ready to be unleashed. As they mold the golden calves they are expected to reject them; as they infuse these calves with spiritual power, they are expected to drain from their creations any transcendental pretense. Avant-garde artists have found themselves both articulators and exaggerators of cultural contradictions as well as agile and sensitive manipulators of the variables that lead to or defuse these same contradictions. Their work is supposed to be both transparent and opaque—and pleasing to the public—at the same time. Can anyone achieve these conflicting goals?

The issues and the examples of artworks discussed in this book try to answer this question. Ours is a quest for recognition of the impossible position into which artists (and scientists, academics, and some political leaders) have been placed without being fully aware of it. Even in the face of Mount Sinai, awaiting Moses' return from his encounter with God, the golden calf was fabricated and worshipped; even in the face of another millennium, golden calves are still being fabricated and worshipped. Ours is not another lament in the tradition of so many nostalgic laments over lost dreams of the past. Instead, ours is a critical engagement with the predicament of contemporary culture and the potential for art to improve the odds of overcoming this predicament.

In order to explain our position, we argue that to substitute art with its discursive residues is to deny the technoscientific and economic conditions that determine the paths of art. We attempt to expose the inherent ambiguities that plague the project of modernity, and therefore also problematize some notions of the historical mission of the avant-garde. In our view, the heightened sense of ambiguity underlying modernity—where bureaucratic and instrumental rationality is accompanied by irrational effects, as in the cases of the gas chambers in Nazi Germany—expands the cultural significance of art and its practitioners, whether or not they are considered avant-gardists. Our approach contradicts that of some postmodern critics, such as Paul Mann, who insist on the role of art in general and avant-garde art in particular to have been successfully resurrected as art criticism and the discourse of art. Moreover, our approach does not subscribe to the view, expressed by Russell Berman, that culture could be the antidote to bureaucracy in the age of modernity, but may

4
◇   turn out to be its "alibi" or counterpart (129). Finally, it also undermines
     the approach of others, such as Christopher Butler, who suggest that the
     critic's role is bridging the gap between "the embattled artist and his
     bewildered audience" (ix), however difficult this may be. In these cases,
     criticism is being substituted for art.

          Our return to art and artworks themselves brings us back to avant-
     garde artists and the centrality of their works in articulating the ambigu-
     ities mentioned above. But when we do this we distinguish ourselves from
     Berman's view of Theodor Adorno's insistence on the obsolescence of the
     avant-garde by declaring the "commencement of a new period, charac-
     terized specifically as postmodern, in which the central elements of the
     project of the historical avant-garde—the emancipation of individual sub-
     jectivity and the radical transformation of the social totality—lose their
     relevance" (Berman 43–44).

          In contrast to this view of the obsolescence of the avant-garde (under-
     stood in its historical context), we appreciate the power of art in general
     and avant-garde art in particular to confront the ambiguities of modernity
     (now in its postmodern guise), critically engage them, and whenever pos-
     sible provide troubling images with which to meet public expectations.

          In redefining the nature of avant-garde art and its relation to modern
     and postmodern capitalist culture (and in particular the complex of eco-
     nomic and technological forces we call commercialized technoscience)
     we reject the dominant notions of the avant-garde. One of those is repre-
     sented by Adorno and the Frankfurt school Marxists who wish to
     empower avant-garde art as a rebellious force against the onslaught of
     capitalism as cultural mass production. The other dominant view of the
     avant-garde is represented by Clement Greenberg and his fellow mod-
     ernists-formalists who wish to cordon off avant-garde productions into a
     spiritual and authentic realm, one that can champion the heroic artist as
     an individualist genius untainted by the commercial truck of a secular and
     greedy culture.

          Both of these notions of the avant-garde fail to appreciate to what
     extent avant-garde artists, like anyone else in contemporary culture, are
     fully enmeshed in the overwhelming powers of the culture of capitalism.
     Being involved in their culture, from our perspective, enables them to
     engage that culture openly and self-consciously, rather than disdain it or
     refuse to participate in it. To some extent, as citizens and artists they can-
     not avoid the culture, find refuge outside of it, since there is no outside

in the age of hypercapitalism, not even the standard refuge sites such as the church or the academy. Avant-garde artists by default, and then by definition, are part of the mainstream, even leaders of the mainstream, who are capable in their own ways of challenging their culture, approaching it critically, and providing new perspectives from which to view it. When they succeed, it is not a display of their complete surrender to the forces of commerce, but rather an expression of their critical engagement with these forces.

Some would argue that one can stand outside capitalism's reach and be truly detached from the cultural engagement of commercialized technoscience. This view is based on some romantic vision (Marxist, no doubt) that capitalism's reach is limited, and that it will break down of its own internal strife. We refrain here from elaborating an economic critique, one that could assess the validity of such a view. Instead, we suggest that under current conditions, and having no evidence to the contrary, we accept the supremacy of capitalism without endorsing its debilitating side effects or its inherent problems with questions of justice, equality, and liberty. We try to steer clear of romantic nostalgia for complete artistic autonomy (the marginal, rebellious genius) on the one side, and absolute distance and detachment from the commercial context (some form of transcendence) on the other.

Our focus on certain conventionally recognized avant-garde artists does not mean that we wish to reappraise their designation as avant-gardists. Our interest in these artists goes beyond their membership in a particular school or movement so that we can concentrate on the distinctive characteristics they display in what we understand and define as their detached engagement with modernity and their continued struggle to meet the intellectual and aesthetic needs of the public at large. They have been self-conscious in expressing, both in their artistic works and in their verbal and written documents, the difficulty posed to them by their culture and its attendant public expectations and tastes regarding the role of art as a response to modernity. Their position is intriguing because they have to maintain their artistic integrity in the face of pressures external to the community of artists, namely, the pressures of immediate gratification through modes of consumption of the present, as Matei Calinescu suggests (7–9). While most critics (Christopher Butler, for example) make out the schism of postmodernity to be between an embattled artist and a confused audience, we suggest that the schism is between the (confusing)

6

◇

material conditions of postmodernity and an embattled community of artists and audiences. Avant-garde artists champion and express the concerns of their audiences, rather than add more concerns to them.

Avant-garde artists have been expected to lead the way out of complacency, suppression, and the acceptance of the status quo and into a new world—as Calinescu puts it: "expressing a self-consciously advanced position in politics, literature and art" (97). Or, as Renato Poggioli argues, avant-garde artists have been expected—as social radicals—to foresee the future calamities of their age, anticipate the cultural misfortunes yet to come, and decry the injustices of the social conditions of their people (9–11). However unfortunate it may be, avant-garde artists, like their commercial counterparts, remain bound by the conditions of technoscience, the marketplace, and media-driven fame, and therefore may never be able to completely break away from their surroundings. In some fundamental sense, they have no escape—just as their audiences are trapped in the information age. In Calinescu's terms (and as a direct critique of Poggioli), the avant-garde response to the conditions of modernity is only one of the "diverse intellectual responses to the problem of modernity," so that "modernism" includes the avant-garde response but is not limited to it (9–10).

Avant-garde artists are not subjects of Marxist or postmodern dismissal, as far as we are concerned, for they are neither the social and artistic antagonists of the elite portrayed by Poggioli, the aesthetic elite of Greenberg, nor the therapeutic healers of Donald Kuspit. We find all of these designations too limited for the actual workings of avant-gardists. Though Roland Barthes may be correct, as Calinescu admits, that in the postmodern age one can no longer prefer any set of criteria against which to evaluate the social and political viability of responses to the conditions of modernity, this does not mean that the avant-garde as a movement is dead (Calinescu 120).

The works of avant-garde artists are at the heart of the cultural stage where the battle over the significance and downfall of modernity is played out, even when their controversial projects add an element of ambivalence and anxiety about the predicaments of modernity. Their detractors and supporters bring to bear issues outside the direct assessment of these projects because of the symbolic quality artworks are supposed to embody, and therefore may fail to appreciate the inherent impossibility of an unambiguous assessment, or the inevitability of complicity amid a revolutionary or emancipatory quest. As Poggioli suggests:

"Even the avant-garde has to live and work in the present, accept compromise and adjustments, reconcile itself with the official culture of the
times, and collaborate with at least some part of the public. . . . Thus we
can say that it is exactly the particular tensions of our bourgeois, capitalistic, and technological society which give the avant-garde a reason for
existence" (79, 107).

Perhaps one way to appreciate the paradoxical position into which
avant-garde artists are put, as Poggioli notes, is to evoke Calinescu's determination of the leadership role undertaken by them while renouncing any
elitist pretensions: "To be a member of the avant-garde is to be part of an
elite—although this elite, unlike the ruling classes or groups of the past,
is committed to a totally anti-elitist program, whose final utopian aim is
the equal sharing by all people of all the benefits of life" (Calinescu 104).

The arts were flourishing at the end of the twentieth century and will
continue to flourish into the twenty-first not despite the avant-garde, the
alleged advanced guard of the militarized and militant cultural campaign,
but because of its fabrication of accessible commercialized aesthetic experiences. It is significant that there is no literary discursive substitution for
works of art that are accessible to the public (whether in museums, galleries, parks, or the popular media). The avant-garde is neither foreign to
nor outside the boundaries of the conventions adopted by the artistic
community in its interaction with the culture at large. It is also not a form
of lament or profound critique of the alienation, exploitation, and antagonism that underlie modern society, as some contemporary theorists—
Kuspit, for example—claim.

Instead, works that we appreciate and would classify as avant-garde
constitute negotiated and compromised artistic expressions that avoid
extreme theoretical positions in favor of a self-conscious critical acknowledgment of the world of commercial technoscience. Avant-garde artists
seem at times to be merely celebrities and the slaves of commodity
fetishism; they are deemed no different from bureaucratic art directors
and technicians. But for us, they reveal the traditional role that artists had
to follow: they had to appease both the tradition from which their works
were inspired and those who funded them, while aspiring to creative transcendence of that tradition and distance from their benefactors. As in the
case of Michelangelo, whether understood as mediators, translators, or
communicators, they were accused of betraying their lofty calling as
much as applauded (post hoc) for their defiant accomplishments.

The avant-garde should not be dismissed as a necessary condition for

8
◇

the perpetuation of bourgeois culture, that is, as a convenient means of knowing the enemy without really being threatened by it. Stalin put these artists in jail; Kennedy brought them to the White House. This view of art in the age of capitalism (Berger) exemplifies and distills the ambiguities that plague avant-garde artists and their creations. Instead of camouflaging or overlooking these ambiguities, instead of pretending that they do not exist (as Stalin hoped) or that they can be easily overcome (as Kennedy thought), we insist that these artists excel at articulating and exaggerating cultural contradictions.

What characterizes the avant-garde artist is the ability to tread a fine line between these options, whether as critic or prophet, autonomous or beholden. Instead of having to choose to be inside or outside the art establishment (which itself is fully ensconced in the commercial establishment), avant-garde artists insist on being both. In their engagement with these establishments, they chart a new course for the mainstream (and not for themselves alone), and they do so knowingly; they expect that the rear-garde will follow and thereby endorse their choices. What makes them interesting in comparison to their counterparts is their struggle to be different and to pose an alternative, however impossible their posture remains.

We selected the examples throughout our text in light of two related issues, technoscience and economics, that we believe help highlight how some avant-garde artists have a detached relationship with the predicaments of modernity. Our selection is intertwined with the history of twentieth-century art, and therefore is limited by the predominance of male artists, especially in the quarters sanctioned as avant-garde. By the end of the century the number of women artists increases, and their representation among avant-garde works increases as well (see, for example, Sherrie Levine's post-Duchamp problematizing of originality and authenticity; Buskirk and Nixon 177–81).

As for the engagement with the intricacies of the financial maze, the romanticized view of starving artists as creative geniuses who are misunderstood in their lifetime and appreciated posthumously is replaced here with a realistic picture of artists as producers of goods and services for which some are lavishly rewarded. Marginalization, according to our view, is misused as a validating criterion for avant-garde status. Michelangelo and Leonardo da Vinci set the tone for modern artists such as Pablo Picasso and Andy Warhol. Artists today find agents and art collectors,

patrons and gallery owners, all of whom differ little from benefactors of
the past, such as popes and aristocrats. Michelangelo set the stage for
avant-garde and commercial artists for centuries to come, having thrived
as he did on commissions from wealthy patrons. His career helped create
the cult of the artist, the celebrity who becomes as well known as his or
her works. Avant-garde artists stand out from the crowd in their ability to
command attention from other artists and the public at large. To accom-
plish this, they must be students and masters of their tradition rather than
rebels and deviants.

As for technoscience, avant-garde artists similarly acknowledge that
the realization of their creativity depends on the use of the latest and most
effective advances of their age, whether they are dyes and canvases or the
marketing devices of the advertisement industry. The technological feats
required for the painting of the Sistine Chapel are magnified in the late
twentieth century when an entire island in the Florida Keys is bordered
with high-tech fabrics (by the Christos). To be knowledgeable about the
latest technoscientific advances demands of the avant-garde a close collaboration with the forces of commerce. In this respect, then, the importance of avant-garde artists is not in the perception of being in the forefront of their artistic community, but rather in their ability to engage the
forces of postcapitalist technoscience.

The dichotomy between art and technoscience in general, or between
what is conceived more specifically as commercial art and the sublime
(low and high art, respectively), collapses in the works of avant-garde
artists. As Sherrie Levine says in an interview with Martha Buskirk: "I'm
very curious about that area where the commodity meets the sublime"
(Buskirk and Nixon 178). Once the notion of the avant-garde artist as an
autonomous individual fighting for enlightenment in the midst of a cultural desert has been suspended, our approach can be appreciated. Likewise, once the notion of the sublime has been problematized by the avant-
garde artist so it no longer is narrowly defined in Kantian terms of
spiritual transcendence or in Jean-François Lyotard's sense of the
"unspeakable," there is greater room for artistic and aesthetic maneuver-
ing. That is, if the sublime becomes a more common experience accessible to a wider audience without thereby becoming mundane, then it will
not remain the purview of connoisseurs whose taste is limited to the gratification of so-called high art.

For example, in order to capture a moment of the sublime avant-
gardists do not escape commerce and technoscience but rather embrace

10

◇ them—without, however, forfeiting antagonism, resistance, and critique. These artists refrain from mockery of commercialized technoscience because they recognize their reliance on these conditions of artistic production, unlike some artists such as Jeff Koons and his enlargement of so-called kitsch objects. Jonathan Fineberg summarizes Koons's artistic turn as follows: "Koons then deliberately moved into kitsch and from there into explicit pornography, making cynical consumer icons for the rich that were nevertheless still more shocking as an expression of his ambition than of his bad taste" (461).

There is an intriguing dialectical tension that may seem to bespeak complicity in the face of the sublime (and that is not as evident in Koons's works as we would like it to be). We argue that this tension or moment is not to be found outside of mundane reality, but in its very core, in the midst of everyday life. Therefore, we focus only on those examples of avant-garde artworks that express this tension, rather than mock it or assume it away. What is dismissed as kitsch, therefore, may play an important role in the dialectical development of taste in the postmodern age, since it foregrounds the significance of artworks amid cultural consumption; and although it is mass produced and commercially consumed, it still contains the potential to heighten the aesthetic sensitivity and sensibility of its audience (Calinescu 225–62).

We do not wish to replace romanticism with pragmatism, but rather replace idealized romanticism or nostalgia with an engaged and critical realism. Even in the most routinized and canonized art forms one can discern ambiguities and anguish. These cracks in the mold of the artistic establishment offer an opportunity for breakage and reconstruction. When avant-garde artists are responsible for this break, they are fully aware of it. This awareness is what leaves them in the mainstream, part of the establishment, and sets them apart as avant-gardists. Some of them even become celebrities. As such, they remain captives of the incessant quest for a nontraditional, nonreligious spirituality that may never be fulfilled. They are Sisyphus-like romantic heroes entreated to be autonomous artists whose genius brings forth novelty and deliverance from the mechanical reproductions of modernity, while they can never fully disengage themselves from the shackles of their tradition and the conditions of materiality (technoscience and commerce).

How can one expect to be an eloquent and successful critic of one's culture if one does not know what is worth criticizing? However much the traditions in fine art have been challenged since Duchamp, the quest for originality and creativity remains intact, and the promise of its fulfillment still entices artists and mesmerizes audiences. The mechanization of human life and its bifurcation into the arts and sciences, as C. P. Snow describes the "two cultures," have done nothing to suppress our longing or satiate our craving for an aesthetic experience that transcends intellectual understanding and ameliorates psychosocial anxiety. In this sense, then, aesthetic awe and inspiration in the midst of hyperreality make even more sense today than before: they are essential social antidotes to cynicism and inhumanity, to what Herbert Marcuse describes as the one-dimensionality of human existence and interaction.

Perhaps because of the great events of the twentieth century—world wars and atomic bombs and the sterilization and medicalization of health and food—there has been an upsurge in public expressions of anxiety over the human condition and the circumstances under which humanity may survive. The unfolding of a new century one hundred years ago was intertwined with the combination of the forces of capitalism, the accomplishments of technological innovations (with the positivism of logical empiricism), and the development of mass production, global distribution, and obsessive consumption (in the neoclassical model). By midcentury the great promises of capitalist technoscience were mired in the devastating results of two world wars, and so lent themselves to the fears and anxieties of Western nation-states. These fears found their voices not so much among politicians and business leaders who wished to extol the benefits of liberty and equality within democracy so as to celebrate post–World War II prosperity, but rather through artists, poets, and philosophers.

The incessant return to the ideals of the Enlightenment throughout the second part of the century, from philosophers (such as Jürgen Habermas in Germany) to economists (such as Herbert Simon in the U.S.), from political institutions (the establishment of the United Nations) to educational ones (mandatory education), is exemplified in the appeal to the mind as a cure for all the ills of the body. The mind—whether understood as human reason, an ordered world view, or a model for rational choice—has at least three types of authoritative institutions or communities to nurture it: religious, technoscientific, and artistic. Leaders and proponents of each of these communities are expected to provide the conditions for survival and success, lend their services to the enhancement of the human condition, and render judgments about the appropriate means of achieving these goals. Reducing all of these into discourses and the

12
◇

power relations that emanate from them overlooks the conditions that brought about such discourses in the first place.

We are scared of neither personal escapism through aesthetic experiences nor the variety of experiences individuals report about encounters with something they would define as the sublime. Instead, we are concerned that if art appreciation is limited to personal and subjective tastes and judgments alone, no lessons can be taught and learned. Similarly, we are concerned that the celebration of the avant-garde as deserving of elimination or of celebrity status misses the point of the problematic position into which a group of artists are thrust, both as custodians of eternal values and profound convictions as well as champions of radical thought and outrageous forms of defiance (against the church and the state alike).

We acknowledge that there is no unmediated experience and that all human activity is theory-laden. Yet, if all human experience is reduced to encounters with discourses, then the sublime is impossible. Put differently, our approach to works of art is social and cultural through and through. To be sure, we focus on the social context of the production, distribution, and consumption of artworks and the status of those designated as avant-garde artists. This is neither to admit the overwhelming importance of artists' motives and intentions nor the unique role of art in our modern and postmodern culture. Art for us remains an important human expression, but not the only one; likewise, it remains an important cultural expression of the state of human activity and social interaction, a way to survey human aspirations and fears.

In order to further our investigation, we focus on specific works of avant-garde art and examine their effects on society. There are several reasons for doing this rather than examining the critical discourses about these works.

First, there is something about art and artists that captures the imagination of contemporary culture in a way that businesspeople do not, but that technoscientists sometimes do. If art is our personal flight of fancy, our way of escaping the mundane for a glimpse of a better alternative, then we cannot allow artists (just as their technoscientific and business counterparts) to become complacent, no matter what practical compromises they feel they have to make.

Second, if the social role of artists is to safeguard us from misrepresentations and the propaganda of politicians (as has always been the case with dissident artists in fascist regimes, for example, the Soviet Union, Italy, and Germany between the two World Wars), then we cannot afford to lose the cultural power they render willingly and openly. The critical dimension provided through the artistic medium is as powerful as the written or spoken word, but has an immediacy and accessibility that elude the friendliest words and speeches.

And third, if we have lost our trust in religious institutions as a means to a spiritual end, and if we still wish to fulfill some form of spiritual quest, then we desperately need art, among other cultural expressions, as an alternative means through which to reach our spiritual destiny.

We add our voice here to many others who value artistic creativity and the fruits it bears, and who have over the years tried to define and explain art and the role it plays in our culture. But when we do so, we refrain from inquiring after the conditions of creativity or the psychological conditions of public reception.

We also remain fully aware of the compromises the artistic community must make in order to master its trade, survive personal hardships, and be heard beyond the confines of its inferno. In this sense, then, our view is not romantic at all: we do not believe in raw talent and individual genius as sufficient grounds for avant-garde status. Rather, we worry about the difficulties that face anyone trying to continue a tradition while maintaining a critical edge and personal integrity in the face of the perplexing complexities of modernity.

Instead of focusing on the aesthetic experience and its inherent subjectivity (Freud) or transcendence (Kant), we insist on the social and cultural character of that phenomenon. In this respect, then, our work falls more comfortably into the domain of cultural studies—where a critical engagement with the limitations of art and the artistic community is paramount—than into the domains of art history and art theory. We believe that if the projects of avant-garde artists are placed in the midst of the so-called mainstream, then their enigmatic character (or radical pretense) can be more readily detected. Although our choice to concentrate on the works of avant-garde artists Marcel Duchamp, René Magritte, Yves Klein, J. S. G. Boggs, Andy Warhol, Keith Haring, and Jeanne-Claude and Christo lends itself to a fairly narrow restriction of art and artworks to the visual, one may expand our analysis to cover many other art forms, such as performance art, music, and dance.

A few words may illustrate what we mean when we confess the narrow focus of our approach. We consider art forms that are neither high art nor advertising, but that contain elements from both areas. If one were to expand our analysis to include avant-garde performance artists, one

14

◇

would include Annie Sprinkle, for example, who acts out and decon-structs pornographic fantasy by, among other things, inviting her audi-ence to use gynecological instruments to examine her cervix. In such per-formances, female avant-garde artists have used gender-related issues to problematize their own relationship to commodification in general and gender-specific fetishism in particular, the exchange of one's body and body parts in the world of commerce, and the objectification (and reifica-tion) of myths, ideals, and fantasies about sex, sexuality, and the posses-sion of the female body.

Though one may argue that feminist critiques of art and the role its practitioners play in the world of hypercapitalism are no more than an extension of age-old Marxist views, we would suggest that there are novel and profound statements feminist artists and avant-garde female artists bring to the fore that may have remained unnoticed by contemporary cul-ture without their insistence. Perhaps one could also elaborate on these issues and illustrate to what extent female avant-garde artists have been able to defy our contention that a detached engagement is inherent in the approach to the predicaments of modernity. We remain open to such a suggestion and set of illustrations.

What makes the artists we examine here and many others of their genre exciting and enigmatic is the fact that their works transform tradi-tional categories and uses of the visual arts, such as painting, sculpture, drawing, or printmaking. Their works cross boundaries and expand and redefine them, exploiting the standard capitalist process of production, distribution, and consumption (through photos or videos, for example).

We appreciate the economic and technoscientific components of avant-garde art inasmuch as they are codeterminants of the critical poten-tial that can be gleaned from these projects. To conclude with some, such as Nelson Goodman, that the languages of art are conventional and there-fore can be understood within prefigured matrices is only the first step for avant-garde artists who wish to supersede these limits. If personal experi-ences (Martin Buber's sense of awe while confronting a tree comes to mind) count as much as and at times overwhelm conventions, can they ever be accomplished outside of conventional languages? The tension between the conventional and the personal, between artistic codes or norms and their defiance, is a crucial element in understanding art, the aesthetic experience, and the role avant-garde art and artists play in our culture.

What may be novel in our approach is the manner in which we categorize avant-garde art in terms of the predicament of artists as conveyors of provocative ideals amidst a system of complacent reproduction (in Walter Benjamin's sense). This predicament was not born in the age of industrial modernity, nor did it die with the emergence of postmodernity; instead, it can be traced to antiquity and will be found in the future as well. The ambiguities and anxieties that beset the culture in general and avant-garde artists in particular are not limited to a particular era; they can be detected throughout history.

Ours is not a call for authenticity (in Theodor Adorno's sense) as a response to the technological age, nor a call for idealized spirituality that escapes religious constraints but maintains promise and hope. Neither is it yet another left-wing attempt to resurrect the avant-garde as the ultimate antidote to the corruption of capitalism, modern politics, and mass communication. Instead, ours is a threefold critique of (a) the misguided appeal to works of art for deliverance from intellectual famine and emotional bankruptcy, (b) any romantic characterization of the avant-garde as resistance and defiance, and (c) the transformation of avant-garde into a Marxist or postmodernist discourse. Once the centrality of avant-garde art in culture is appreciated, then its study will illuminate the anxieties underlying all cultures.

Though one may read our text within the framework of postmodernism, and although we would agree that postmodernism enhances the understanding of modernism, our argument should not be dismissed as yet another postmodern attempt to level the artistic playing field. When we choose particular works as examples for our theoretical constructions, these choices can be defended according to a set of criteria. These criteria are themselves open to questioning, but they all contribute to our appreciation of the special character of some avant-garde pieces of art. One can follow our criteria and extend the variety of examples, one could change some of the criteria, without undermining the gist of our argument, namely, that there is a critical dimension in some avant-garde pieces that illustrates the predicaments of modernity during the twentieth century.

For example, when we review some of Warhol's pieces, we are less interested in his blurring of the lines between high and low art and more interested in his insistence on the business conditions under which art is created and distributed. Warhol's conscious deliberations over framing his pieces, reproducing them, or marketing them indicate his sensitivity to rather than defiance of the economics of art. Likewise, his critical

16
◇   engagement with the various mediums available to his commercial counterparts links him both to his artistic ancestors and to his contemporary
commercial and graphic artists. We make similar claims about Duchamp
and others, but remain silent about the case of women artists since for
most of them the main issue during much of the twentieth century was
the validation, legitimacy, and acceptance of females as artists equal to
and at times different from their male counterparts. The economic
dimension of their position was dwarfed by comparison since they represent such a small minority of the total number of works and their prices.
(The Guerilla Girls' poster "The Advantages of Being a Woman Artist"
[1987] highlights the fact that one painting by Jasper Johns fetched more
money than would have been enough to purchase the works of sixty-eight
women artists, a group that includes most of the renowned women artists
of the Western world.)

Let us add a few more words to explain why our work does not have
a sustained discussion regarding the marginalization of female artists in
twentieth-century avant-garde circles (limited, as we acknowledge, to the
visual arts). First, there is an economic reason for our choice of artists.
We wish to illustrate the capitalist appeal and seduction that overwhelm
and compromise the critical approach of artists, and this has been more
the case with male artists than with their female counterparts. Female
artists have been less likely to be seduced by commercial appeal, because
they have been outside of that commercial loop, so to speak. In some perverse sense, then, female artists could retain a more critical approach in
their works, a more detached engagement with their cultural context.

Second, performance art as a strategy for opposition is a response
from the margins, from outside the artistic establishment, to the extent
that this art form is neither for sale nor collectable. This takes female per-
formers such as Annie Sprinkle and Karen Finley (the chocolate-covered
woman), who are unabashedly critical of the commodification of female
bodies and therefore refuse to flirt in any way with the capitalist male gaze
(since they expose its overt aggression, violence, and predatory nature),
completely outside the avant-gardism that is the focus of our attention.
That is, there is no ambivalence or obfuscation in their artistic expressions; there is no complicity in their critique; it is straightforward, confrontational, and lacks the self-doubt detected in the works we examine.
In this way they are no different from male artists such as Joseph Beuys
and Vito Acconci.

Our sense of artistic detached engagement in relation to so-called celebrity artists among the avant-gardists should not be construed as an endorsement of their critical faculties. Instead, we realize that in many cases they, too, fail to retain their respective detachment from the seduction of commercialized technoscience; but that makes them more, rather than less, interesting, for their predicament is ours as well. Our choice of artists and their works is not construed as a way of admiring their exemplary courage; rather, it shows the many cracks in the community of avant-garde artists.

We should add that we avoid the definition and social value of art in order to highlight the precarious position into which artists have been placed in the afterglow of modernity, when Auschwitz, Hiroshima, and other calamities of World War II overshadowed some of its benefits.

As a historically informed book that focuses on the dialectical practices of the avant-garde in a critical manner, this work falls more readily into the category of a cultural critique rather than an explication of aesthetics. For example, Hilton Kramer claims that the avant-garde has degenerated into simply the tradition of the new and novel. The authentic quality expected of artistic works has been eliminated; what is found is only a mountain of hype. Kramer's lament fails to account for the self-conscious moment in avant-garde presentation: these artists are celebrating their impossible task of responding to the predicaments of modernity. Is it the content of the artwork that's new, or its mode of presentation? Can anything be novel, or is everything nothing but footnotes to the wisdom of the ancients, to paraphrase Alfred North Whitehead? Is originality definable? Is creativity limited by what the Greeks understood as mimesis (mimicking the old)? To be new or novel assumes that there is a tradition already in place, and that the new or novel is outside that tradition. This view leads to a twofold paradox: first, the new is new only in relation to something else and in that sense is never fundamentally new, and second, the minute the new is recognized as such it becomes old.

Similarly, Clement Greenberg claims that the avant-garde plays the role of self-critically defining the core values of artistic mediums. His own role as critic, then, is to outline the formal progress of these works, and thereby characterize them as avant-garde. By doing so, he ignores the dialectical complexity of the avant-garde that makes it impossible to render it essentialist. We appreciate the difficulty of trying to characterize the avant-garde without committing to a definite and easily recognizable set of features. In this respect, then, any claim concerning the avant-garde is

18   bound to be essentialist on some level. What is worrisome about Green-

◇   berg's claim is the formal progress it subscribes to the avant-garde, as if it
follows a linear trajectory. Our concern here is to show that avant-garde
artists followed different routes and dealt with different issues in their
works. This makes their identification much more difficult for art historians and critics, yet no less intriguing.

To some extent, we agree with Peter Bürger, who suggests that the
avant-garde reintegrates art with culture, so that its criticism must
include self-conscious examination of the social and political role of
artists and their works. In this fashion, then, the avant-garde, no matter
how seemingly varied and incomprehensible its expressions, remains
grounded in the foundation of the culture despite its attempts to overcome or heal it. The dialectical tension that this situation brings about is
what fascinates us and gives rise to the general public's frustration with
the avant-garde. The interesting feature that permeates avant-garde works
is the struggle of their authors to deal with at least two sets of issues that
complicate their role: technoscience and commerce. The artists we
observe here deal directly with these matrices in their works, their interviews, their lives.

In what follows, we present a grid of sorts and examine in some detail
certain artists and their respective engagement with these matrices. There
is no precise order in which to read the chapters; they all treat similar
concerns of modernity but with different examples. For example, the
question of money, financial institutions, and the relationship between
the independent artists and the world of commerce is more pronounced
in the cases of Klein and Boggs than in those of many other so-called
avant-garde artists. The questions of public accessibility, the reward for
the artist's (free) labor in producing the projects, and the appeal to public or private funding undermines a simple-minded resolution to the
predicaments confronting avant-garde artists. How can artists benefit
monetarily from their works, while claiming absolute independence from
those who pay their bills? Avant-garde artists are at their best not when
they escape this predicament, but rather when they confront it head-on.
When they do so successfully, they are capable, as Klein and Boggs show,
of disorienting not only their community but the entire culture.

The avant-garde is a component of modern culture, a component
whose artistic instantiations vary from generation to generation and from
region to region. The variations diffuse the potential for a single definition, but they do not veil the persistence of the avant-garde as a cultural

and social medium through which the predicaments of modernity can be assessed. An informative cultural critique should pay close attention to the avant-garde as being at the center and not on the periphery of cultural representations and enduring values. In this sense, then, the avant-garde is not necessarily at the cultural forefront prefiguring cultural values (in Marshall McLuhan's sense). Instead of searching for novelty and originality or theoretical rigor, one should unveil the ambiguities, anxieties, and anguish that lie at the heart of contemporary culture and perpetuate the avant-garde at its core.

We concede that even when avant-garde artists proclaim themselves to be radical visionaries, their works fit neatly into a tradition. One may call this the tradition of resistance or the tradition of being untraditional; no matter what it's called, it is still a compilation of precedents that accumulate into a critical tradition. It is with this in mind that we coin the term *the tradition of defiance*. This is not the age-old defiance of the establishment, but rather the defiance of being labeled avant-garde or not. To be avant-garde is to be simultaneously a radical artist and a traditionalist, a dissident and an accomplice. The concern with critical defiance fits well into what we consider to be ongoing avant-garde encounters with commercial technoscience, because these encounters are critical. They are critical in the sense of a detached engagement and not as mere resistance or rejection; there is no full embrace, either. And finally, they are meant to permeate the culture, taking the public seriously, and fabricating golden calves.

1

Romancing Science and Technology

The machine stripped bare by her bachelors, even as she is clad
in full armor.
                    —Cicotello and Sassower, with apologies to Duchamp

Introduction

THE PROVOCATIVE works of Marcel Duchamp and René Magritte
reveal the enigmatic courtship of the machine by avant-garde aesthetics. The art and lives of these two important visual artists of the early
twentieth century provide useful examples for our assessment of the role
science and technology play among the values we find central in artistic
production in general and avant-garde art in particular. The analytic-
minded Frenchman Duchamp was an acclaimed "anti-artist" whose paradoxical "ready-made" art was informed by the radical technique of using
unaltered, manufactured objects as the basis of his visual statements. A
guiding light of the rebellious, anti-establishment European dadaists as
well as the (pre–World War I) American avant-garde, Duchamp enjoyed
an active social life and attained celebrity status among the elite in his
adopted city of New York.

Magritte, by contrast, was a socially modest Belgian whose mundane
"bon bourgeois" life style and conventionality of artistic technique belied
the outrageous behavior typical of his fellow members in André Breton's
surrealist movement. He painted images of everyday objects in traditional
oils rather than selecting them from the shelves of hardware stores, as
Duchamp did. However, Magritte shared Duchamp's fascination with the
enigmatic displacement of the commonplace. The perplexing juxtaposition of mundane objects in his images dramatically problematizes their
recognition by a viewer since he insists on the essential relativity of the
phenomenological world. Coupling these two seemingly disparate artists
allows us to validate certain themes of the avant-garde that we find central

22 and persistent. Among them are the romanticizing of science and tech-
◇ nology; the troubled fascination with the power of the machine; the
"beauty" of the machine's progeny—the mass-produced object; and the
detached engagement incumbent on the avant-garde artist as a critical
shield against absorption and loss of self.

Ours is not a nostalgic recollection of the glorious defiance of European artists at the dawn of the twentieth century or of the lament that
accompanies the rise of modernity and the downfall of utopian aspirations. The critical assessment of the avant-garde position in relation to the
themes of technoscience and commerce is too often used to either casti-
gate or embrace works of art and thereby define them in particular ways.
In either case, the analytic discourse often highlights narratives of originality, rebellious posturing, and formalist credibility as the core values of
aesthetics. Such narratives are not the concern of our analysis. Instead,
we insist on reassessing artists' paradoxical use of science and technology,
commerce, and media-driven commercialized art in order to better understand the cultural context of the avant-garde at the dawn of a new century.

What makes avant-garde art informative to the concerns of contemporary culture is the response some of these artists provide in the age of
commercialized technoscience. Enjoying the fruits of the scientific revolutions and the financial and industrial dominance of capitalist modes of
production, Russell Berman suggests, "it cannot be denied that avant-
gardism has contributed significantly to a profound reorganization of culture by integrating these previously excluded domains [commodification,
exploitation of nature, and popular culture] into the realm of art. . . . The
construction of the bourgeois institution of [fine or high] art is no longer
plausible once neither the contrast between high art and low art nor the
difference between culture and nature can be maintained" (50–51).

Some examples of avant-garde works of art and their conventional (or
orthodox) interpretations can clarify our focus. Surrealist images such as
Max Ernst's *The Murderous Airplane* (1922), Man Ray's *Object to Be
Destroyed* (1936), and Alberto Giacometti's *The Captured Hand* (1936) are
among the many expressions of twentieth-century avant-garde artists
describing their disenchantment with modernity and its mechanized life.
The hope, in this case, is for transcendence from technoscientific modernity via "la révolution surréaliste" that André Breton called for in his man-
ifesto. The critique of early twentieth-century industrial culture implied
in these works is in most respects unambiguous: these artists see what

Walter Benjamin sees (the age of mechanical reproductions), and they fear that this prophetic pronouncement is not limited to their represen- tations but can engulf the entire culture.

The theme of artistic disenchantment in the face of modernity is understood in a more sophisticated way by avant-gardists, according to Thierry de Duve, who realized that even the use of paints in tubes changed the craftsmanship of the artist into a skill of a laborer. As he says: "Mechanization and division of labor have replaced the craftsman in most of his social and economic functions, so why would they spare the painter? Indeed, to cite but the most blatant specific impact of industri- alization on painting, from the moment photography was invented, painters have lost their job as purveyors of resembling images . . . the product of their labor had to compete with a cheap ready-made substi- tute" (148).

Duchamp explains in 1961 his reaction to the modern conditions under which artists work, shifting their sight from traditional painting to assem- blage work, in the following way: "Since the tubes of paint used by the artists are manufactured and ready-made products we must conclude that all paintings in the world are 'readymade aided' and also works of assem- blage" (ibid. 163).

As we shall see in the case of Duchamp, even more so than with Magritte, their critiques are related to technology and its tools of repre- sentation, as well as the attendant Freudian concern with the balance between the reality and the pleasure principles. A tradition and its history and an entire world view are under siege, not just their descriptions or inscriptions. The alleged technoscientific pessimism of these artists often has been canonized in historical analyses as the ultimate expression of what constitutes legitimate avant-garde content, as if one could ever por- tray it in a critically linear fashion. All of these examples betray what con- cerns us, namely, a more complex and problematic view of human entan- glement and obsession with technoscience, a lament laced with admiration.

It also makes sense, from the perspective of technological disillu- sionment, that the surrealists and their predecessor dadaists speak today to a worldwide audience larger than the tiny avant-garde communities in the major metropolitan centers of their historical origins. In spite of being the most notorious and enigmatic artistic movements in the early twenti- eth century (using familiar objects juxtaposed to unfamiliar scenes), the

24
◇ surrealists and dadaists quickly became celebrities whose works today are reproduced by the millions (to hang in every bourgeois home) and anthologized in books (carried by every respectable library). Many of these artists have been incorporated within a decade or two into the contemporary "industry of fakes" and as source material for record album and CD-cover art, a telling marker of their cultural presence and immanence in contemporary life.

Dadaists and surrealists in general provide an avant-garde platform every neo-Luddite can join, namely, the rejection of the mechanization of the life-world. This rejection or lament effectively depicted by other artists, such as Charlie Chaplin in his film *Modern Times* (1929), becomes the battle cry of the first half of this century. What conventionally defines these avant-garde artists as radicals is the utopian dimension and spiritual transcendence that are always in the background regardless of the dystopian façade they put up. The critique of modernity is romanticized! If only science and technology were in the hands of artists and not engineers, we could enjoy a better world and a happier future!

Our intent in this chapter is not so much to fight the established characterization of avant-garde art as a champion of resistance to the overwhelming encroachment of industrialization, but rather to tease out certain themes that will expand the notion of the avant-garde and its cultural involvement with science and industry. The works of Duchamp and Magritte are of interest because they are more enigmatic than others of their period: they do not present a conventional avant-garde either/or approach to modernity and its implementations. Theirs is not a rejection of technoscience, but a selective choice made in the face of its persistence. Moreover, these works exploit the dichotomy between utopia and dystopia, between mechanical reproduction and spirituality, between lament and celebration, between commodification and the quest for the sublime. For these artists, there is no easy way out: one must carefully choose how to tread a fine line between two equally frightening abysses. Finally, if they contribute to a cultural critique it is in the form of detached enchantment, fragile harmony, and tentative equilibrium.

Science and Technology

According to the Marxists, capitalist technoscience is both alienating and exploitive; it dehumanizes our daily activities. The prescription was revolution and not religion (the opiate of the people). State Marxists devised political agendas as strategic implementations; humanist Marxists hoped for social and moral transformation through universal education; liberation theologians prayed for the church to help bring about the equality of the Kingdom of Heaven in a socialist or communist format here and now. What social vision is left for avant-garde artists in a Marxist culture? If they happened to be working during and after the revolution in the U.S.S.R., some became the productivists who designed workers' uniforms and housing so as to further the revolutionary agenda of the politicians. Others went underground so as to retain the critical and spiritual flame that the Communist Party was crushing. In both cases, one can trace the Enlightenment ideals of rationality, equality, and liberty as the informing principles and driving forces behind their artistic creations.

Small wonder that many early twentieth-century avant-garde conceptions reflect an acknowledgment of the technoscientific gods. Once the Enlightenment and modernity as we know them make their influence felt throughout the Western Hemisphere, no one can remain indifferent to science and technology. Technoscience invades every facet of human life, from personal hygiene to the infrastructure of transportation, communication, and dwelling environments. Some recipients of technoscientific fruits become technophiles, while others become technophobes. The hope and dread associated with different experiences and expectations of technoscience overwhelm the artistic community as well. That is, artists cannot afford to remain indifferent to technoscience (even if they could; and as Duchamp claims they cannot—see his example of the paint tube), whether they use new tools and materials or criticize the infatuation with technoscientific instruments such as the locomotive, bicycle, and propeller. Any unilateral retreat to a natural state is counterproductive; it is self-defeating utopianism.

One could mention in this context the acrobatic photography of Margaret Bourke-White. Around 1935 Oscar Graubner photographed her perched within a gargoyle on the Chrysler Building, literally in the skies above New York City, grasping her movie camera. She stands out because this image combines, in a powerful manner, her exploits with machine images in her photography and the juxtaposition of her own image within the photograph. Whether she is standing on the ground or hundreds of feet above within the projecting ornament of one of the most famous architectural icons of urban modernism, her artistic statement parallels that of Duchamp to the extent that she insists on the aesthetic beauty and pleasure that inanimate objects can have and evoke in the modern imag-

26
◇

ination. Moreover, if one's imagination is to soar to the technologically accessible heavens, so to speak, what better way to do so than to be depicted thrust out into space near the top of what was then the tallest building in the world?

What is fascinating about avant-garde artists of this era is their implicit, and at times explicit, confession that they must deal with science and technology. Implicitly, one can parallel French cubist aesthetic concerns with multiple perspectives in what may appear as traditional still life or nonmechanical paintings with the burgeoning physical theories of quantum mechanics and relativity. Explicitly, Italian futurists embrace in their written manifestoes, poetry, and visual art the power, speed, and dynamism of the industrial revolution with direct reference to the workings of motors, engines, and automobiles. To quote Duchamp: "People living in the machine age are naturally influenced, either consciously or unconsciously, by the age they live in" (Kuh 90). In short, avant-garde artists of the turn of the century are conscious of their own situation vis-à-vis technoscience and feel compelled to respond to the *Anger of the Gods*, as one of Magritte's works (1960) is entitled. What might the gods be angry about? Is it the way in which humans have lost their humanity and aspiration to divinity? Or is it their loss of a self-image that is modeled after an image of God? The emergence of technoscience disrupts the direct link between humans and God; it adds a dimension that mediates and has the power to transform that very mediation. In fact, the centrality of technoscience in the twentieth century diverts humans' attention from God and divine revelation. But unlike with God, there is no sacred text of a superior machine that reveals the secrets of the divine. There is no path one is ordained to follow.

What, then, is the status of technoscience? Technoscience is inherently unnatural; that is, it establishes a dichotomy between natural and unnatural objects, between the constraints imposed by nature and the means by which to defy or overcome them. Though the divine is separate from humanity, it provides ample links (through Jesus, Buddha, or Allah) for overcoming this divide. But how does one cross the divide between the natural and unnatural? How does one classify a wheel, or more specifically, *The Bicycle Wheel*? Is placing it where the hand can spin it (as Duchamp did in this "assisted ready-made" of 1913), rather than where the foot can push it, a defiance of the mechanical intention? Is this a deliberate way of reinventing the wheel and therefore an attempt to waste time and energy in the face of efficiency and productivity? Is this a perverse hearkening back to the age of the spinning wheel—and of the loom? The loom uses natural fiber, wool, to keep humans warm, while the wheel converts human walk into human ride. Though the wheel admittedly is unnatural (an artifact of human creation), its raw materials are found in ores underground; that is, in nature. What about an artist's brush, or paints? What about the wooden frame on which a canvas is stretched? On which side of this divide between the natural and artificial, or between the spiritual and the technoscientific, does the avant-garde stand?

Duchamp subverts these questions by acknowledging that there is no choice to be made here in regard to a nostalgic view of the past, when the tools of the artist and the skill with which they were used had an individual signature ascertained by the viewer. The tools have changed in the modern age and so have the skills, and in order to appreciate and cope with these changes the artist must adjust to a new world view. Duchamp suggests in an interview in 1963: "A readymade is a work of art without an artist to make it, if I may simplify the definition. A tube of paint that an artist uses is not made by the artist; it is made by the manufacturer that makes paints. So the painter really is making a readymade when he paints with a manufactured object that is called paints" (de Duve 163).

As de Duve explains, Duchamp's brilliance is in realizing early on that the conventions of art and art history themselves were to be reevaluated, and therefore understanding his avant-garde orientation and expressions to be ones that challenged traditional art and art history (303). Duchamp subverts the Kantian paradigm of aesthetic judgments by pointing out the conflation of theoretical concerns and practical conditions of modernity as a more fruitful way of dealing with the classical separation between reason (and rational judgment) and emotions (sense perception and taste) (314–15).

Avant-garde artists such as Duchamp and Magritte seem to refuse to make a simple choice that would push them to either a romantic refuge in the past or the soapbox of apologists and promoters of the latest technoscientific feat. Instead, they seem to keep a paradoxical detached engagement with technoscience: they are critics who feel compelled to face the predicament of their age. If anything, they can be accused of being opportunists: this predicament is a motivation, a provocation, and a stimulation. Every mechanical device they observe turns in their hands into a potential recollection of its predecessor and successor. The

28 mass-produced car is juxtaposed with the natural horse, the smoking
◇ steam locomotive to the wood-burning fireplace, the metal bicycle wheel
to the wooden stool. No object remains outside a context—historically,
logically, and materially.

The viewer is forced to reflect not only on the human condition in
general, but also on her or his own experience with and exposure to these
mechanical objects. Duchamp and Magritte force their audiences to
make a personal judgment about objects that seem inconsequential and
deemed unworthy of serious consideration. Only when framed as works of
art do they become worthy of intellectual reflection, emotional contemplation, and critical speculation. From our perspective, the very framing
of these objects, their "arrest" within the frame, is a necessary device for
a moment of soul-searching. The frame is of course an artificial device
that arrests the natural continuity of space and time. The arrest can be a
framed painting, the designation of an object as "art," or the selection of
one frame in a film (as Magritte does). From this perspective, one can
clearly appreciate the enigmatic character of film: is this modernist inven-
tion that tries to emulate natural continuity capable of producing an
arresting moment?

Avant-garde artists who hold our interest distinguish themselves in
playing the role of enigmatic framers, knowing full well that what they
offer their viewers will prompt a question accompanied by a tentative
answer. They refuse to frame an answer, in contrast to the prophet or
preacher who gladly supplies ready-made answers (right off the shelf of
the software library). Despite their reluctance to provide answers, and
perhaps because of this reluctance, they end up finding themselves in yet
another predicament: isn't their art in fact a moralizing exercise in some
sense? One could argue with Nietzsche that though their works have a
purpose, it is not a moralizing one. On the contrary, the purpose may be
to undermine the unquestioned authority of the preacher and his message. As Nietzsche says: "The struggle against *purpose* in art is always a
struggle against the *moralizing* tendency in art, against the subordination
of art to morality. . . . When one has excluded from art the purpose of
moral preaching and human improvement it by no means follows that art
is completely purposeless, goalless, meaningless, in short *l'art pour l'art*.
. . . Art is the great stimulus to life" (92–93).

The orientation expressed in avant-garde art clearly defines a goal, a
purpose, an aim for which art is produced and consumed, for which there

is a motivation to take risks and set oneself up for public scrutiny, critique, and ridicule. The celebrity status acquired by avant-garde artists is post hoc and accidentally so; rarely does one have the power to become a celebrity on one's own. Instead, the purposefulness of one's work catches the cultural eye and heart of a people, and before one is able to anticipate it, there is a wildfire that consumes an age, that burns in the midst of the desert, that turns an artist into a cultural icon.

It would be irresponsible for anyone living in modern times to ignore the consequences of technoscience, whether they be the evils of pollution and overpopulation or the advances in biochemistry that have doubled life expectancy in fewer than two hundred years. In this respect, then, our focus on Duchamp and Magritte as two avant-garde artists informed by technoscience should seem less perplexing: they turn out to be not radicals who provoke for the sake of provocation, but rather responsible citizens who worry about the welfare and future of humanity. It should be noted here that the influence of technoscience on these artists is twofold. It informs their choices of what to frame, what to focus on, what to single out of the entire industrial cornucopia, as well as how to do so, whether through Duchamp's mechanical drawing style that is reminiscence of engineering and architectural blueprints, or Magritte's flattened, posterlike illustrations of objects. In both cases there is a deliberate rejection of traditional fine-art techniques for creating three-dimensional illusionism (chiaroscuro or photo realism) in favor of an approach that references a world of commercial life before the exalted spirituality of high art.

The enigmatic features of these works of art—their detached engagement—readily suggest the characterization of their creators as avant-garde artists: first, the accessibility of the images (daily life, commonplace objects); second, the ambivalent focus on science and technology (romanticism meets modernity); third, the monumental status of objects such as the bicycle, automobile, telephone, watch, fireplace, umbrella, and all other mundane ready-mades of industrial production and capitalist consumption once framed. Who hasn't seen a urinal, or, for that matter, Duchamp's *Fountain* of 1917? Who doesn't know what it is? So, how can it ever turn into a work of art, acquire a monumental status? According to Duchamp: "Whether Mr. Mutt [Duchamp's pseudonym] with his own hands made the fountain [in fact a factory-made urinal] or not has no importance. He CHOSE it. He took an ordinary article of life, placed it so

30 that its useful significance disappeared under the new title and point of
◇ view—created new thought for that object" (*The Blind Man,* May 1917;
quoted in Schwartz, 283).

Extracting a urinal from a public bathroom or a hardware store and
placing it in a gallery or a museum disturbs the uniform world view that
separates the natural from the manufactured, the aesthetic from the com-
mercial/industrial. Duchamp's "creation" was the framing, the placing,
the title, and the perspective. But in order not to obliterate the disturbing
effect of the urinal at the gallery, Duchamp insists on some form of alienation: he speaks of himself in the third person.

Magritte's painting *Personal Values* (1952) places images of personal
effects—comb, match, bar of soap, goblet, shaving brush, bed, armoire,
and area rugs—in a framed blue skyline with white clouds, as if they were
in a glass display that belongs in a museum rather than in a bedroom.
While seemingly creating a scene of carefully defined naturalistic images,
Magritte distorts and disrupts our conventional appreciation of these
ordinary, useful objects. The disproportionate sizes of these manufactured
artifacts and their placement in the composition challenges our prefigured, stable relation with our daily surroundings. Can the depiction of
everyday products be transformed into an awe-inspiring monument that
transcends their identification with commercial value and practical reality? Has Magritte created a "new thought for these objects"?

What fascinates these artists and their audiences are the cultural
changes mechanical devices undergo through history, and the potential
for transformation, even transgression, that art affords them. When
Duchamp and Magritte propose to use their trade and skill for a particular case, when they juxtapose the ordinary with the bizarre or the mundane with the magical, they hope to provoke some self-reflection and even
social action without a prescribed ideology of the left or the right.

In our view, then, accessibility to a general public is obvious. It is not
difficult to appropriate and reproduce as posters and record labels, as
symbols and clichés, the anxiety felt by the public. Who is not delighted
by the automobile, while remembering the good old days of horseback riding on the family farm? Who does not romanticize about the past, knowing full well that the present cannot be given up? Who doesn't want the
fruits of technoscience without having to pay their debilitating price?
Duchamp and Magritte play into the hands of their public, pose the
dilemma so well rehearsed by others, delighting their viewers along the
way with cheerful colors and seemingly comfortable images. Theirs are

neither the pessimistic jeremiads of the surrealist technoscience naysay-
ers such as Ernst and Giacometti, nor the utopian images of Dali's landscape of drooping watches. Instead, they retain their dignified distance
from an answer, while pressing on with the daunting and unnerving questions: What is one to do about technoscience? About life?

Anecdotes

At the height of the early twentieth-century cultural fascination with
the newly emerging mechanical devices and gadgets, an interesting event
takes place, one that has become legendary in art history lore. An endnote
numbered 116 in K. G. Pontus Hulten's *The Machine as seen at the end of
the mechanical age* says the following: "Quoted in German, without original source in exhibition catalogue *Fernand Léger,* Munich, Haus der
Kunst, March–May 1957, p. 31." With this reference, the reader is already
attuned to the mystical character of what is being quoted. "Without original source" is an aberration in scholarly texts, a way to explain that one
cannot know for sure who is reporting the incident. Was it really the
French artist Fernand Léger who said what is quoted there? Or was it
made up after the fact by those who wished to present the situation in a
particular way? Here is the quote:

> Before the World War [I] I went with Marcel Duchamp and
> Brancusi to an airplane exhibition [the Salon de l'Aviation]. Mar-
> cel, who was a dry type with something inscrutable about him,
> walked around among the motors and propellers without saying
> a word. Suddenly he turned to Brancusi: "Painting [fine art as we
> know it] has come to an end. Who can do anything better than
> this propeller? Can you?" He was very strongly attracted to these
> precise objects; we were also, but not so overwhelmingly as he.
> . . . But I still remember the bearing of those great propellers.
> Good God, what a miracle. (140)

Let us consider first the cast of characters: Léger was an adamant
promoter of machine aesthetics as the only viable basis for contemporary
art. His 1924 film *Ballet Mécanique* integrates classical aesthetics with the
grace of mechanical movement, accomplished in the triumphant new
technological medium of artistic expression, the cinema. He also is the
author of "The Machine Aesthetic, the Manufactured Object, the Artisan

and the Artist" (1923), which celebrates the beauty of machine forms. It is
he who recalls the exchange at the aviation salon, he who ends the quote
with an exclamation about the "miracle" of the propeller.

Constantin Brancusi, who is hardly mentioned in this story beyond
his presence, is himself an important artist whose sculptural forms reflect
a predilection for, and an emulation of, machinelike finishes. His works
look as if they were mechanically made, yet are curiously all handcrafted.
Shortly after this legendary meeting, Brancusi begins a three-decade-long
preoccupation with a propellerlike series of sculptures (the "Bird-in-
Space" theme).

By contrast, the third character is not as one-dimensionally obsessed
with machines. Yes, it is attributed to him the great fascination with the
machine; but that is as much a projection of his fellow visitors, as psy-
chotherapists would call it, as a single-minded concern of his. True, he is
the one who challenges the two others to do "anything better"; true, he
laments the decay or disappearance of fine art; yet, he challenges them as
well, motivates them to pay close attention to mechanical production and
the complexities inherent in any act of (art) appreciation. But the attention he demands goes beyond superficial admiration and "love at first
sight." We would quickly add, did they get it? Do those who quote the
incident get it?

While Léger and Brancusi can be identified as technophiles, even
though Léger is more extremely a promoter and Brancusi a reluctant participant in the romantic approach to machines and mechanical production, Duchamp is clearly the provocateur, the instigator of a challenge,
the critic who incites radical rethinking of the very notion of fine art. But,
as quoted earlier from Nietzsche, there must be a purpose for this aesthetic provocation, there must be a goal. What is Duchamp's goal? What
does he find fascinating in the propeller? Can it even be an art form, an
expression of human creation and the life we lead?

In our view, Duchamp illustrates the ambivalent position into which
technology has thrust his generation. In the skies of the early twentieth
century the propeller moves airplanes in the air, replacing the lovely, chip-
pering birds of sentimental landscape pictures, replacing the graceful
images of the handheld fan as the device with which air is moved by
humans. Propeller-driven aircraft transcend the bounds of nature as the
romantics portrayed it; they are harbingers of threat, doom, and death, as
the two World Wars will show the entire European continent. Duchamp
cannot dismiss the propeller just because it is in one salon as opposed to

another: the Salon de l'Aviation is no different in cultural importance from the Salon des Beaux Arts in Paris or the provinces. If anything, the centrality and gravity of the technical exhibit halls take on a disproportionate larger stake in the life of modernity; they replace the focus of attention; they dominate cultural discourse. They do not re-present anything outside themselves; they present themselves as they "truly" are, as objects of use and of multiple admiration, for their graceful usefulness and their inherent beauty. They inform the avant-garde.

For Duchamp, then, it is a logical extension to move from the single propeller, taken out of context from the machine it propels, to the ready-mades, those objects that retain their utility despite being removed from their context. The urinal (*Fountain*, 1917), for example, is shocking in a way that the propeller is not. Why? Perhaps because the propeller has no pretense to represent anything but itself, while the urinal is placed by Duchamp at a fine art exhibit, pretending to be a work of art. Can it be? Would one have the same reaction if Duchamp had placed a propeller at an art museum? What would the authorities have said?

There is an interesting anecdote about such cultural confusion. When the photographer Edward Steichen bought a Brancusi propellerlike "Bird-in-Space" sculpture and brought it with him to the U.S., customs officials refused to admit it as legally duty-free art and insisted it was a machine part requiring customs duty. When the case went to court in New York City, Brancusi had to testify by affidavit from Paris that he had made this piece of art/machine with his own hands. Of course, he had to be authenticated as an artist and not a machinist (by affirming that he made no objects of "utility" or "reproduction"). Customs officials were the litmus test of what one considers art in the middle part of the twentieth century. Perhaps Duchamp's prophetic statement about the end of fine art was true: all that is left are beautiful or ugly machines, provocative or destructive machines.

A similar anecdote can be told about Duchamp's own studio and the upside-down bicycle wheel stationed on a wooden kitchen stool, ostensibly as a "distraction," in his words. What is at issue when people recall this artifact in the artist's studio? Was it a fascination with an old wheel— a wheel of fortune, a roulette wheel, a Ferris wheel, a bicycle wheel? Was it the tranquility that a revolving wheel brings to the chaos of the artistic imagination? Was it nostalgia for days gone by when the automobile was not yet invented, when humans powered the machine rather than motors? Was Duchamp restoring some lost factor in an equation? All of these questions we answer in the affirmative, because we see him as one of the last openly romantic artists.

Staring into the abyss of the technological sublime, Duchamp inadvertently postures himself in the manner of those early nineteenth-century romantics staring into an environmental abyss. In both cases, one is confronted with awe and dread, not knowing which emotional response will carry the day. The propeller is for Duchamp an emotional experience as powerful as any sublime craggy mountaintop or thundering cascade.

The height of bicycle culture was in the mid–1890s, when Duchamp was about ten years old; a decade later, the automobile takes over at center stage of urban culture. By the time Duchamp makes the gesture of legitimating a mechanical device, the bicycle wheel, as an object of aesthetic value alone (disregarding its use or exchange value), the bicycle has lost its cultural centrality as urban transportation. Duchamp's gesture is romantic and critical at the same time: his lament is laced with respect and ongoing fascination. Unlike Picasso's *Bull's Head* (1943), constructed from a bicycle handlebar and seat, which inverts and converts machine parts into an animal narrative and submerges the alien into the familiar, Duchamp's *Bicycle Wheel* is not transformed—it is what it is, a wheel that still turns aimlessly.

Picasso's image is about power, wherein the bull plays into the mythological and historical preconceptions regarding an uncontrollable natural force, arrested and tamed only within an artistic framework. The analogy between the bull and the machine is clearly depicted in Picasso's work, so that the power of the machine substitutes for the power of the bull. The machine is a natural and evolutionary progress from the raw power displayed by the bull, so that to consider a machine a bull, if you will, makes perfect sense to the viewer. Just as the bull is feared, sanctified, and sacrificed at the altar of religion, so the machine bull is turned into a worthy icon feared, sanctified, and sacrificed at the altar of technology. Are they both untamed and wild, out of control? Or can one simply frame the bull and the machine, control them the way Francis Bacon hoped science could control nature? These questions inform modern science and the ongoing march of technoscientific modernity. What distinguishes Duchamp as an avant-garde artist is his depiction of machinery as if it were unnecessary to undertake symbolism, in comparison to Picasso's loaded symbolism and his refusal to chart a way out of the predicament of modernity.

Duchamp does not join in Brancusi's transcendental approach to the propeller as a bird or Picasso's bicycle parts as a bull, nor does he fetishize the machine as if it were the latest and best nude one can find, as Léger does. Instead, he has this to say about his ready-made sculpture: "When I put a bicycle wheel on a stool, the fork down, there was no idea of a readymade or anything else. It was just a distraction. I didn't have any special reason to do it, or any intention of showing it [in a gallery or museum], or describing anything" (Cabanne 47). This quote, taken literally, illustrates the denial of the transcendental, a refusal to see beyond the real. But can Duchamp say this in the face of the Nietzschean insistence that there is no "thing in itself" but only the interpretation of interpretation? Can the human mind be devoid of intention altogether? That he did not nor could have anticipated this particular gesture to prefigure an entire genre of ready-mades is true enough; yet, this only confirms Duchamp's status as an avant-garde artist, one whose fascination and lament combine into a creation that provokes an entire age, while using that age's simple, daily artifacts.

On another occasion, Duchamp says the following about his bicycle wheel: "To see that wheel turning was very soothing, very comforting, a sort of opening of avenues on other things than material life of everyday. I liked the idea of having a bicycle wheel in the studio. I enjoyed looking at it, just as I enjoy looking at the flames dancing at the fireplace" (Schwartz 442).

This quote captures the theme we try to articulate here, namely, the enigmatic, detached-engaged relationship with technoscience. The wheel replaces the flames; regular mechanical revolutions replace random bursts of fire; the predictability of the circular motion eases the tension that accompanies the threat of irrational flames. The fire is tamed with the turning of the machine, the threatening heat is subdued by the fire engine, rolling on its way to suppress the danger and potential disaster. At the end of the day, Duchamp sits by his fireplace, now consisting of a bicycle wheel he whimsically turns by hand. Does his spinning wheel fan the flames of technology? Is he soothed by the turning of the wheel of fortune? Can modernity answer these questions? Can it incorporate the old and the new, the mechanical and the magical? Where has he placed his bet?

Magritte continues this Duchampian denial of any easy replacement of one form of soothing nostalgic musing with technology's siren call. Fireplace? What is that in today's world? It no longer serves to heat houses, but rather becomes an object of decoration, luxurious contem-

36 plation, and leisure entertainment (it's now the centerpiece of the living
◇   room, not functioning in the kitchen or bedroom anymore). What comes
out of the fireplace of modernism, if it isn't heat or soothing flames? How
about a smoking locomotive! A piston-driven machine emerging out of a
walled fireplace is as incongruent as the now common replacement of
wood-burning fireplaces with gas-heated imitations using artificial logs.
One of nature's oldest and most cherished experiences is being jettisoned
in the mechanization of the industrial age. The campfire of the home is
now controlled; its messy aftermath is neatly eliminated; nature is steril-
ized in bourgeois households. Ashes have turned into stainless steel.

As Magritte said in a lecture in Antwerp (1938) when describing a
group of paintings that juxtaposed flames with inflammable objects such
as rocks, tubas, keys: "The Discovery of Fire [series] gave me the privilege
of experiencing the same feeling as has been felt by the first man who produced a flame as the result of banging two stones together" (quoted in
Meuris, 82).

Is it possible to emulate and recall the experiences of nature and of
natural phenomena through artificial aesthetic images? Can one replicate
one set of feelings with another? Magritte seems to suffer from the same
pretentious posturing as many of his contemporaries, comparing his discovery to that of the first man who produced fire. What about
Prometheus's theft of fire? Is the artist a discoverer or a thief from the
gods?

Though Magritte claims to discover, it may be more accurate to claim
that by the early twentieth century all one can do is recover, uncover, and
perhaps steal from the past. Magritte himself steals the known images of
a tuba and a flame (The Discovery of Fire, 1936) and a burning piece of
paper, an egg, and a key (part of The Ladder of Fire, 1934), just as he has
a locomotive emerge from a blocked fireplace on whose mantle one finds
rigid, undrooping, and empty candlesticks. Is no flame possible in this
world, in this frame? Or, is this a rejection of the obvious, of the inevitable
and expected flame of the fireplace, the candles, and the locomotive? Is
his a lament or a death sentence? Does he endorse or reject the march of
technoscience?

Perhaps Magritte's attitude toward technoscience can be gleaned
from his aircraft paintings, depicting what he calls "Black Flags" (1936 and
1937). When Magritte paints these flying machines, they are neither
utopian images that recall Icarus and his transcendental quest to soar
toward the sun, nor typically surrealist dystopian complaints about the

dehumanization of machine-powered motion and transportation. Though historically displayed at the height of the surrealist movement, they defy the programmatic and conventional-pessimistic response to technology typical of this movement. (See, for example, Max Ernst's *Murderous Airplane* and *Peaceable Swan*.) Magritte's planes are curiously powerless: they have neither propellers nor engines to move them along. They are elegantly designed geometric figures that are composed of household items, such as windows and plumbing pipes, balls and planks.

Whether these images are set against a dawn or dusk background, they all express what Milan Kundera calls the "unbearable lightness of being." They perplex the viewer and challenge one's conception of what airplanes are in terms of their use value. They look more like kites and gliders than the powerful and potentially destructive machines they have become. To imagine them as tools of annihilation is ludicrous; to imagine them as pilotless aircrafts is equally silly. These seem to be useless (they show no potential for setting a trans-Atlantic record or dropping an atomic bomb); they seem so aloof as to ignore the economic and militaristic demands put on technoscientific discovery. Instead, Magritte's images transform the terms of the debate and demand of us an aesthetic appreciation of lightness and flight. Is there something beautiful about the airplane and our perception of it? Is it sublime when it floats in the sky? Can we turn down the noise and clean up the mechanical mess of living under the flight path? Magritte must be aware that his juxtapositions, the steaming locomotive going nowhere out of the fireplace (it seems stuck in mid-air) and the mysteriously suspended aircraft moving no one, are intended to provoke, question, and challenge. They certainly perplexed his fellow surrealists, as the following example shows. E. L. T. Mesens complained in relation to Magritte's "Black Flag" paintings: "Poetry? Circumstantial magic? A revolt against the state of reality?" (Hammacher 110). Since Magritte is avant-gardist in our sense and not in theirs, and since his enigmatic response to technoscience gives no clear indication of his attitude toward technoscience—he appears to be neither a technophile nor a technophobe—it is little wonder that a conventionally minded surrealist such as Mesens would be confused and even outraged. Where does Magritte stand? Do his personal values, ideological commitments, and cultural expressions tell us what his view is?

The answer might be found in Magritte's *Personal Values* (1952), the image of conventional objects in a startlingly enigmatic context mentioned earlier in our discussion. The scene in this painting is of some typical per-

38 ◇ sonal effects placed in an oddly decorated, windowless bedroom. The proportions of the articles are baffling: a huge goblet, a gigantic shaving brush and comb, a match the size of a bed, an armoire in scale to the bed but too small to store a nearby bar of soap, all placed neatly against cloud-painted walls or walls that are transparent to the outside scene (both readings are valid). Alexandre Iolas, an art critic sympathetic to surrealist ideas, on 15 October 1952 wrote to Magritte about this particular image: "It disarms me, it throws me, it leaves me confused and I'm not sure whether I like it. Be an angel and explain it to me." Magritte wrote back a week later, trying to be an angel: "A painting that is truly alive should make the viewer feel ill, and if the viewers do not feel ill it is because 1) they are too coarse or 2) they are so used to feeling ill in this way that they take it for pleasure" (Meuris 140).

What may be to some playful confusion or puzzling juxtaposition makes others feel ill at ease. Confusion turns into illness, the critique into an indictment. For Magritte, the world comes to life through an introspection about mundane objects that are mechanically produced and endlessly reproduced on an assembly line. Therefore he claims that for a painting to be "truly alive" it must make its viewer "feel ill." There is an intention in Magritte's work, a purpose, as Nietzsche claims, a reason for which the carefully defined images are framed in a particular fashion. Magritte, like Duchamp, presses ahead in his quest for the appropriate questions that need to be asked in light of the pervasive power of science and industry. But his quest is bound to be misunderstood by those who are searching instead for clear-cut answers. His "personal values" are those of the paradox of detached engagement with technoscience. The enigmatic avant-garde is his purpose, his desired goal.

Even the controlled stability of this still-life painting of his personal effects, items that he needs for his daily routine and therefore have value for him, is challenged by the inclusion of an oversized pink match. The brightly colored match seems to exist only to be struck and consume the entire enigmatic bedroom, the entire frame. The fire of modernity is now controlled by matches, those simple devices that transcend the ancient limitation of banging two stones together. Yet, can it ever be fully controlled? Is this the ultimate dilemma of contemporary technoscience? Has Magritte joined Duchamp in observing and commenting on the predicaments of their age?

We believe that both Duchamp and Magritte have overcome the limitations of their fellow critics by rejecting the simple dichotomy of art and science, creativity and repetition, originality and assemblage, nature and simulacre. For them, the machine is an extension of human activity, of the direct link between the creations of nature and our technology. For instance, how is one to classify fire? Is it a natural phenomenon or a harnessed element that is manipulatable and in turn manipulates nature in the name of tranquility and human happiness? It's not that Duchamp and Magritte love to hate the machine or that they appropriate the machine in order to destroy it. Instead, they venerate the products of technology and offer diverse methods of worship.

Money

Happiness can be measured in ways as diametrically opposite as self-sacrifice and deprivation for a lofty goal and opportunity for leisure and extravagance. Because of these two extremes in the human continuum of moods and aspirations, there have been two major myths in the romantic (or avant-garde) artistic community. The first relates to a conception of the artist as an impoverished, misunderstood genius whose solitary and uncompromised accomplishments are eventually acknowledged by society. The second concerns the traditional relationship between artists and financial, religious, and political leaders, wherein the expected generous patronage would provide artists unfettered opportunity for expression within the confines of their benefactors' tastes. These myths and the cultural patterns that gave rise to them have been shattered in the face of capitalist production, distribution, and consumption. To follow Marx in this context, art and artifacts have been commodified, commercialized, and fetishized.

Duchamp, Magritte, and the rest of the avant-garde artists we consider here cannot hide in their garrets, nor can they expect to find the church or the state as their patrons. Instead, they must seek the good grace and taste of capitalists. It is interesting to note how each of them engages the capitalist reality. Just as they embrace science and technology and the industries related to them, so they embrace the trappings of capitalism. Yet, as avant-garde artists they do so in what we call a detached engagement: they simultaneously accept and deny the importance of money. For example, in 1919 Duchamp went to his dentist in Paris, Daniel Tzanck, and gave him a drawing of a check in lieu of payment. While a bank note is legal tender between two parties sanctioned and governed by the laws of the state, what Duchamp gave as payment is obviously a

40 forgery: it is enlarged (8 1/4" × 15 1/16"), hand drawn, designated in dollars
◇ rather than francs, and "drawn" on "The Teeth's Loan & Trust Company
Consolidated" of 2 Wall Street, New York.

Any exchange is consummated when the two parties agree as to
which items are to be exchanged. In this case, the dentist accepted an
obvious forgery as a form of payment, while Duchamp intended to give
away a drawing and not actual money. Why did Duchamp do it? Was he
mocking the banking industry? Was he trying to demonstrate that his
money was worth as much as normal money? And why did the dentist
accept the drawing? Did he have enough real money and was glad to have
a piece of art? Or did he hope that Duchamp's money/art would increase
in value, unlike regular money? Obviously the two thought their exchange
was mutually beneficial: Duchamp got his dental work paid for and was
able to make his point about his financial credit and the commercial
power of a critically acclaimed artist, while the dentist enjoyed a greater
rate of return for his dental work. In 1964, in his essay "26 Statements re
Duchamp," John Cage agrees with the significance of this exchange by
singling it out as one of Duchamp's six most important productions
(Judovitz 75).

Dalia Judovitz has a different take on this exchange. She reminds us
that the dentist was also a collector of contemporary art. For him, the
check was definitely a work of art and not a mere reproduction of a monetary bill, a check. She concludes by challenging her audience to "wonder
whether the Tzanck check does not represent his own 'drawing up' of a
document/work whose intent is to legitimize his particular interpretation
of art: one where the will and testament of art is defined by its symbolic
expenditure" (171). As far as Duchamp is concerned, his own work is spent
because it leaves his hands, it no longer belongs to him. But when he
trades it, relinquishes his possession, he receives something in return.
(We discuss issues related to exchange and use value further in chapter 2.)

Duchamp, as we see, toys with the cultural norms of his day, challenging the banking industry as well as those professionals who charge
fees for their services. Checks as we know them today originated around
1781 in the United Kingdom when notes and deposit receipts were
replaced with checks and checkbooks. The attempt to bring back a barter
economy in defiance of the commodification of capitalism—the anony-
mous check drawn on a bank instead of a handwritten I.O.U.—is of
course romantic. It tries to return to center stage the person who is

involved in the exchange, the person whose teeth were treated and who must pay for services rendered with eggs, a bushel of corn, or a drawing. If Duchamp were a farmer, one could expect a chicken, perhaps, rather than a drawing.

There is an additional avant-garde twist in this story. Duchamp's drawing is not a drawing in the traditional sense, even though hand drawn, since it is a replica of what may be considered a check or bank note. The dentist may not know how to respond: a check one deposits in a bank; a drawing one hangs on the wall. If he frames this particular piece in a traditional way and puts it on the wall, will it elicit the expected aesthetic response that a landscape drawing or a portrait would? But what is he to do if the local bank will not "cash" this "check"? The dentist agrees to see past aesthetic misgivings or practical needs and appreciates the ambiguity of what he is given: it is and it is not a drawing, given to him by an artist-patient. Duchamp also agrees to see past aesthetic conventions or practical needs: he can afford to pay the bill, but chooses to draw instead.

But Duchamp's lament over the loss of artistic purity in the face of the overbearing powers of capitalism is itself half-hearted, almost ironic. Picasso was more than eager to doodle on a napkin in a restaurant and give it in exchange for his meal. For him, barter was simple: a meal for a signed drawing, one form of production for another, one form of creation for another, and finally, one form of consumption for another. But what kind of a doodle counts, or does it not matter at all? Is it the signature that one values, that can be exchanged? If such is the case, why not focus on one's signature and not on one's work? If it's a signature we are after, why not simply ask for a signed check? That is what Duchamp proposes: here is a signed check, and it's "my" check in more than one sense. When contextualized in this fashion, Duchamp seems to concede to the romantic ideal of personal exchange of "personal values," adding the word "Original" on his drawing of a check. Even though it has the image of a mass-produced drawing, he lends it the commercial authority of an original, unique, and authentic work of art.

Another story that illustrates Duchamp's detached engagement with commerce covers a long period of his life. For many years he was an adviser to art collectors. Not only was he promoting his own works for sale, but he was convincing patrons of the arts that buying and owning artworks would be financially beneficial as well as an indication of their

42
◇
aesthetic insight (and, on occasion, foresight). If artworks are perceived as an investment and not merely objects for aesthetic fascination and enjoyment, then capitalism has managed to commodify everything human. Why would an accomplished artist turn down lucrative commissions from art dealers in order to advise others what to buy or sell? Perhaps Duchamp was interested in challenging the lines of demarcation between the producer, distributor, and consumer of art: he now becomes not only the producer (the artist) but also the agent for distribution (Brancusi's and others' art) who influences those who are about to consume this particular commodity (private collectors and museums).

Many of his works, what he produces for the marketplace of aesthetic objects, turn out to be not his creations at all. Instead, they are ready-mades easily found in stores and markets. One could argue that the question of the signature looms here as well: aren't these ready-mades (such as urinals, bottle racks, and combs) nothing more than vehicles for putting his signature on, adding value to seemingly valueless objects? At the same time, the minute they are signed by Duchamp, they cease to have their regular use value; they have become valuable in a different way. With one gesture of the pen, Duchamp can lay to rest, reclaim, and paralyze an entire industry. The power of one human, a Nietzschean übermensch, transforms the conventional view of the marketplace. While most critics focus on Duchamp's challenge of the art world, we insist that his challenge is interwoven with a great deal of mastery, manipulation, and endorsement of the framework within which modern commerce takes place.

To be an avant-gardist in Duchamp's sense, then, is to engage with one's immediate artistic community as well as with the culture as a whole. It is fairly easy (though still courageous) to upset the rules of the artistic community by, for example, entering a urinal into an art show. It is far more difficult to challenge the financial community and its powerful guardians by producing personal checks and displaying commodities in inappropriate places. Only if you are sufficiently established and powerful enough to stand on par with your potential benefactors (agents, managers, brokers, and buyers) can you seductively transform the conventions of the day. Are Duchamp's ready-mades a Nietzschean commentary on the problematic position of re-presentation (never quite capturing the "real" or the "thing-in-itself") or an advertisement? Does he try to undermine the lofty position of artworks in the minds of viewers, or does he try to elevate daily objects to the position of contemplation and desire? In either case, his statement is about the blurring of artistic boundaries and the boundaries of consumption. If modern life and human relations are predicated on consumption and material exchange, why would anyone presume that art objects can be exempted? For Duchamp, obviously, any such attempt is futile.

Magritte is at home in the commercial world just as he is in the artistic community. For him, as with Duchamp, the world of commerce is both enticing and revolting. He manages to participate in this world (managing an advertising firm with his brother) by producing posters, commercials, and films, making money for himself and his clients, while remaining an artist who shocks and disgusts as much as entertains his viewers. He refuses to be limited to one domain, one area of production and consumption; he defies the boundaries that try to separate the commercial from the artistic worlds. In doing so, he alerts his viewers to the artificiality of categories, boundaries, and frames (however useful and necessary at times). That the convenience of framing should not be mistaken for validity or legitimacy is foremost in Magritte's aesthetic conceptions.

What Magritte does so eloquently is frame his enigmatic images in ways that are simultaneously accessible to a wide audience and awe inspiring in their paradoxical implications. Take, for example, any of the many versions of his image of a pipe floating above a bold graphic inscription that reads in French "THIS IS NOT A PIPE" ("The Treachery of Images" series, 1926–66). Note the following: First, typically advertisements combine a visual image with a verbal text, a title, a statement. Second, the specific pipe depicted in the painting is readily available from local vendors, it is mass produced and widely used; at the same time, like all pipes, it is something personal that one holds in one's mouth. Third, the pipe is framed in a way that at once elevates it into an object of aesthetic value (with an appropriate caption) while retaining the quality of an advertisement (the caption is directed at an audience).

All of these issues and questions are raised the minute a pipe is framed, the minute the framed (now useless) pipe is displayed in public, that is, is displayed in a gallery or frame shop. Magritte's brilliant critique is not about the pipe itself, but about the cultural context within which a person perceives it. Instead of writing cultural and linguistic critiques of contemporary society (as Foucault does, for example), Magritte simply does them all within one image, with the strokes of a brush. The confinement of the frame, the arrested moment displayed on the wall, is both limiting and challenging. How can one bring to life so many issues within

44 one frame? How can one express a detached engagement? The deliberate
◇ use of familiar techniques and materials (and subject matter) provides the
important recognition factor necessary for the viewer of his paradoxical
expression. The twist of framing a captioned image of an object alerts the
viewer/reader to the uncanny character of this not-quite-an-advertisement
fine-art poster-painting. As much as the twentieth century has been driven by capitalist commercialism and the incessant quest for greater consumption, Magritte wants to challenge any academic demarcation
between so-called high and low art. By leaving the pipe alone with a caption he is questioning the methods of legitimation when a work of art is
framed and formally displayed.

Our fascination with Magritte in regard to the particular challenges
expressed in his works is explicable in terms of our fascination with particular aspects of the avant-garde. The avant-garde, as we explained earlier, is not about being different or rejecting the norms of the artistic community, but rather about the detached engagement with technoscientific
modernity so well applied in works of artists such as Magritte. Magritte is
no different from Duchamp in this respect: technological feats (including
reproducible daily articles of consumption) deserve critical scrutiny.
Magritte creates a fine art poster, a detached engagement with the commercial world. In doing so, he acknowledges the inextricable relationship
between the fine artist and the commercial artisan. He neither rejects the
prospect of making a poster or a commercial nor adopts an alleged critical attitude that scoffs at anyone who would adorn beer bottles ("Painted
Bottles" series, 1937–41).

Similarly, Duchamp took an existing advertisement for Sapolin brand
house paint—a little girl painting a bed—and with paint altered the
graphics to "Apolinère Enameled" (1916–17). He used new paint to alter
an actual advertisement sign about paint into a piece of art, thereby turning it into an item worthy of framing, in the fine-art sense. (Incidentally,
advertising images from periodicals of the past are being collected nowadays.) In their respective ways, Magritte and Duchamp both legitimate
the engagement with conventional capitalism while maintaining their elevated cultural status as artists (critics) whose detachment allows them to
enjoy a perspective different from the one espoused by commercials.

The commercialization of contemporary culture is undertaken by
marketing agencies who skillfully transform everyday objects and human
desire into consumable objects (commodities). What distinguishes the
apple on the tree or the sand on the beach is their framing within the mar-

ketplace, where food and leisure time are bought and sold. The right packaging can make an ordinary object appealing, seductive, and desirable so that it is associated with an image, fantasy, or social status and therefore can command a price no one would have paid otherwise. The process of selection, isolation, configuration, and display when packaging a product or a service parallels the process of framing by artists.

It seems that Magritte is more concerned with frames and framing than with what is inside the frame. Sometimes he uses the frame to exclude or include certain aspects; on other occasions he salutes the frame, as when he draws on the bottle as a whole and thereby turns the container, the package, into an art object in itself. Likewise, it is unclear what to make of his nude paintings. Are they about the plight of women, or about their aesthetic beauty? Is he mocking the commodification of nudity, or is he peddling soft pornography? Are women advertising tools when their bodies are chopped into pieces, as in Magritte's *The Eternal Facts* (1930) or when they are contoured-framed, as in his *Representation* (1937). As any marketing novice will tell you, adding a bit of sex, violence, and death is a sure way to attract customers.

High/Low Art and Celebrity

One of the distinctions of avant-garde artists is their self-proclaimed right, even audacity, some would say, to decide how to challenge the boundaries of high and low art. Their choices for focus and reproduction, their decisions about what to isolate and elevate, betray a level of arrogance reserved for cultural leaders. What makes the Magrittes and Duchamps of this world into celebrities? What elevates them in the public's mind to a status reserved for a small elite?

As far as we are concerned, avant-garde artists well deserve such elevation. First, these artists are careful observers of public tastes and preferences and are astute enough to portray them in the most familiar fashion conceivable. In doing so, they play into the hands and minds of their audiences and thereby minimize the alienation factor that enters into the relationship between the artist (the talented genius) and the average person. In finding a common denominator, such as the wheel, and celebrating its beauty and functionality, the artist legitimates the daily choices individuals make (such as riding a bicycle or spinning wool).

Second, the public is always suspicious of the art community and its pretenses, posturing, and auras. When artists speak to their audiences rather than over their heads, some form of communication is possible. The use of familiar items and ideas, from household objects to eroticism and violence, seduces the viewer into taking a look, stopping and contemplating the most mundane of daily observations and experiences. The inducement to reflect in an irreligious context (the artists we consider most provocative are not preachers telling people what to think or do) provides a comfort zone different from that of communal praying.

Third, avant-garde artists reclaim a wider territory of aesthetic experience than usually expected by a saturated consumer society. Can a bottle be beautiful regardless of its content? Can the very contours and shapes of a bottle, chair, or wheel inspire one's imagination? As far as the avant-gardists are concerned, the answers are always yes. They become celebrities not so much because they lead but because they turn into spokespeople for the legitimacy of everyday life. One need not go to the sanctuary of the museum to appreciate fine art; any house will do.

Finally, the celebrity status of avant-garde artists is achieved through an innocent (and deceptive) posturing that invites identification by the public. If all they do is reconfigure everyday life, their gesture seemingly doesn't require the God-like creative genius of the Michelangelos of Western artistic culture. If I am no different from them in experiencing everyday life, then I can be just like them. If I am not, it's because of my deliberate choice to remain aloof or disengaged compared to their obsessive insistence on engagement. But if I only wanted to focus on a wheel, pipe, bottle, soup can, or T-shirt, I could do it as well as they do! Or could I? Would I successfully elicit the reaction of the viewers of detached engagement so endemic to avant-garde artists?

In our later chapters we will develop the theme of detached engagement as it relates to the overall cultural matrix within which artworks are produced, displayed, and consumed. From our perspective there is a continuity in aesthetic conviction between artists, their agents and brokers, gallery owners and managers, collectors, and public audiences. A suspended disbelief engulfs the process of art creation and appreciation, so that no one is quite sure what value to assign to a piece of art. We will also discuss the issues of money and celebrity raised in conjunction with our analysis of the avant-garde's relationship to technoscientific modernity. More specifically, the next chapter focuses on the financial issues surrounding and infused in the artistic community, while the chapter that follows it will spotlight the celebrity status of avant-garde artists.

None of these topics exists in isolation within avant-garde art, but the particular works of art and specific artists we will be analyzing have been chosen to emphasize each of these factors. Not only is there no reason to believe in the death of the avant-garde, but it is precisely that element in the artistic community that is the bloodline for its survival. The avant-garde moves from the familiar to the bizarre, weaving its way carefully and critically, without much fanfare and offense, seducing as much as provoking, asking questions as much as providing answers, enmeshed in the predicaments of technoscientific commodification.

2

Consuming Art as Commodity

Thou shall not press down upon the brow of artists this
crown of thorns; thou shall not crucify artistic creations upon
a cross of gold.

—Cicotello and Sassower, with apologies to William Jennings Bryan

Introduction

THE QUESTION of money, financial institutions, and the relationship between avant-garde artists and the world of commerce is more often than not obscured in a haze of rebellious posturing and ideological disdain. For as long as art has been culturally appreciated and elevated to a central role in the consumption of leisure time and expression of religious spirituality, it has had an underlying reality of commodification. That artists were always paid money or gold for the production of works of art—their fabrication of golden calves, as we call this process—has become increasingly evident. But what was not as evident until the twentieth century is the fact that artworks are not limited to the aesthetic enjoyment of their owners, but instead become yet another investment whose profitability is measured like any investment in other commodities. The questions regarding public accessibility, the reward for contemporary artists' (free) labor in producing speculative projects for consumption, and the appeal to public or private funding undermine a simple resolution to the paradox posed here: how can an artist benefit monetarily from her or his works while claiming absolute ideological independence from those who pay the bills?

Avant-garde artists are at their best not when they escape this predicament, but rather when they confront it head-on. Yet, this confrontation cannot be simply a self-conscious gesture loaded within established academic discourses, but the kind of confrontation that is recognized as a critique or a critical engagement. This is what we alluded to in chapter 1 when we coined the phrase "detached engagement": the deliberate attempt to resist the temptation of complacency when one is fully involved with and aware of one's complicity in maintaining the conditions of postmodern capitalism. Under our conditions of observation, there is an inherent ambiguity in what qualifies a work as avant-garde: is it its confrontational position or its creative appeal—or both? When Yves Klein and J. S. G. Boggs, the two avant-garde artists examined in this chapter, display their works that comment on the artist's inescapable relationship with commerce, they are capable of disorienting not only their close-knit artistic community but the entire culture: there is a warrant for their arrest!

One may further appreciate the problem of the intricate link between art and money when attempting to define works of art. Is anything with aesthetic value considered art? Is a beautiful sunset a work of art? Must it be represented (the image and the product—a two-tiered sense of representation) by an art dealer and sold for either money or other goods in order to be an artwork? Are we admitting that aesthetic value is less of a defining characteristic than exchange value? What about the individual who paints but never shows the painting or sells it? Is the painting in and of itself an artwork? These are not idle questions, since many bona fide artists have become "artists" only posthumously (Van Gogh, for example). According to Tristan Tzara, "art is dreams that money can buy" (Peterson 66), and as such, then, dreams and aesthetic relics are art only when money buys them. This may seem a radical departure from more openended definitions that allow anything to become art when so deemed by someone (museum curators, critics, theorists) making a good argument on their behalf, a process one may call the cultural sifting of artworks.

Of course, any clear-cut boundary between artworks and other inanimate objects is bound to elude the keen observer of cultural phenomena. One's utensils one day are someone else's artistic creation another (in Marcel Duchamp's hands an everyday kitchen gadget, the bottle dryer, is projected to the status of a work of art; following this early example, Judy Chicago's banquet table with its specially designed dinner plates has been promoted to the level of an artwork by galleries and museums). As we will discuss in the next chapter, this delineation encompasses also the distinction between so-called high and low art, where the former is undertaken for aesthetic value alone and the latter is contaminated by commercial pressures and the conditions of its production, distribution, and

50
◇

consumption. As we saw in chapter 1 (in the case of Magritte), the blurring of such distinctions was already under way in the early part of the
twentieth century: the production of advertisements and canvases for
bourgeois consumption was in the hands of one and the same artist. This
blur undermines the ability to distinguish between conventional and
avant-garde art as well: what was yesterday's avant-garde art is tomorrow's
conventional or forgotten effort, and vice versa.

Unlike art projects of the Renaissance past that had the patronage of
popes and Medici princes, and therefore the endorsement of individual
wealth (see Goldberg), twentieth-century artists have been portrayed by
the Frankfurt school (Theodor Adorno and Walter Benjamin) as becoming increasingly captive to the capitalist age of mechanical reproduction.
Challenges to and mastery of the cultural chain of artistic production, distribution, and consumption will be illuminated here as one of the features
that characterize the fascination with and definition of the avant-garde. Is
it possible in the postcapitalist, postindustrial, post-postmodern age to
eschew any financial contamination? Is it possible to create art for art's
sake so as to inspire aesthetic awe and maintain a credible and critical distance? What would be avant-garde about art in the capitalist world?

In what follows, then, we reconfigure our analysis of the avant-garde
as it was set in chapter 1, because here the emphasis is on the financial
conditions of the art world rather than on the historical precedents and
the context of artworks as critical expressions of the scientific and technological developments of the twentieth century. Structurally speaking, in
this chapter we focus on the economic matrix (the status of artworks within
the capitalist mode of production, distribution, and consumption), while
keeping an eye on the technoscientific matrix outlined in chapters 1 and 3.

The Exchange of Aesthetic Value

Historically, one may reconstruct a presumed division between aesthetic value (or what constitutes beauty) and commercial value (or what
constitutes commodity value and ownership). During the Renaissance,
popes and Medici princes helped codify and formalize this separation
between art as commodity and as awe-inspiring artifact by zealously collecting artworks so as to display their wealth and distinguish themselves
from their fellow citizens. The added benefit to this establishment of collections was that it took the art out of circulation. The notion of collecting art and keeping it as a "one of a kind" item creates a valued status that

is difficult to assess in simple monetary terms. Add to this the fact that displaying artworks in churches and palaces implicitly elevates and sanctifies them, and what quickly and inadvertently developed was a more radical split between aesthetic value and exchange value than ever before in history.

Economically, one may describe the role of artworks post-Renaissance in the following terms. Once artifacts were taken out of the regular process of commodity exchange, their value could not be simply regulated by their sale prices. Once a pope paid for a piece of art by Raphael and took it out of reach of any other potential buyer, the value of the piece was assumed to be higher than originally paid. At the same time, that particular piece was no longer evaluated in monetary terms, but as a piece with aesthetic value different from (usually higher than) its exchange value. The artwork ceases to be a commodity, it is now an object of beauty. But will it be worshipped like a golden calf? Will it attain an iconic status transcending its golden weight and graven image? Of course, any acquired status is as long- or short-lived as its owner's desire to keep it out of circulation. Once a collector decides to sell a valued possession, it is immediately a commodity once again: its value is determined by the price someone is willing to pay in the marketplace. Such a work is perceived as an investment tool from which profitable future exchanges can be made.

Though we limit our discussion to aesthetic production and highlight some artworks of avant-garde artists, one could expand our analysis to include other "texts," other modes of cultural production. We follow here the (leftist) insights of Russell Berman, who makes the following claims about the commodification of all cultural productions: "it should be clear that the capitalist literary production—the culture industry—is not simply a matter of the popular literature of mass distribution. Rather, in the age of organized capitalism, the categories of capitalist production are reproduced in all literature, since all texts, high and low, are caught in the same society of commodity exchange and reification" (69).

Within this context, it is helpful to return to Georg Simmel's analysis of the transformation of and delineation between the use value and aesthetic appreciation of human products, offered at the dawn of the twentieth century: "So long as objects are merely useful they are interchangeable and everything can be replaced by anything else that performs the same service. But when they are beautiful they have a unique individual existence and the value of one cannot be replaced by another even though it may be just as beautiful in its own way" (74–75).

52
◇
The utility of objects and their interchangeability legitimates the monetary value attached to their exchange; but this is not the case with objects whose original utility and subsequent reification have become obscured because they no longer have immediate use value. Simmel explains how the (subjective) individual confronts and is confronted by the process of economic exchange, so that the objects being traded already incorporate an objective standard according to which their value is set at particular time and place: "the objects circulate according to norms and measures that are fixed at any one moment, through which they confront the individual as an objective realm" (79). Aesthetic value can be either "reduced" to the level of "objective" market exchange (where money is the final measure of worth) or "elevated" to the level of a collectible museum piece (where connoisseur taste extracts it from circulation). Once a museum piece re-enters the marketplace it acquires an objective value, the price one is willing to pay to purchase it.

It is noteworthy to follow this process of the shifting status of artworks between commodities (material artifacts) and spiritual icons (transcendent mediums), because it highlights the very definition of art and artworks. What makes an inanimate object a piece of art? Whether or not one agrees with Simmel's analysis, the idealistic attachment to the notion of art as the sublime or transcendent has been constantly challenged since the Renaissance. If one reduces the answer to "a person created it," then any tool could be an artwork. (Exploring this possibility seems to be why Duchamp was fascinated with everyday industrial products, as we saw in chapter 1.) If one reduces the answer to "it is a divinely inspired product," then a poem and a meal could be artworks. (But would this answer not thereby reduce all art to religious artifacts and thereby to religious dogma and belief?) If one reduces the answer to "it has an intrinsic aesthetic value," then one is left with another question: "but who determines that value?" And here we are back to the definition of aesthetic value and its status in relation to the exchange value of artifacts and all other human-made creations.

John Berger, in contrast to Simmel, argues that aesthetic value is enhanced by the perceived or real value that an artwork has in the marketplace (23). Extracting art from the marketplace, as the popes and the Medici princes did, does not increase its value (because of its authenticity and unattainability) but rather its actual participation in the circulation of marketplace exchanges. Artworks in this sense are therefore representatives of their culture and the period of their production, and the more visible they are, the more valuable. But what do these pieces of art represent? According to the Marxist analysis of Berger, "The art of any period tends to serve the ideological interests of the ruling class" (86). The ruling class wishes to present itself and its operations in particular ways, and by commissioning and purchasing only certain works of art it exerts control over how it is represented in perpetuity. Berger continues: "Capitalism survives by forcing the majority, whom it exploits, to define their own interests as narrowly as possible. This was once achieved by extensive deprivation. Today in developed countries it is being achieved by imposing a false standard of what is and what is not desirable" (154).

Berger's concern echoes Marx's disgust with the fetishism of commodification and the ability of the owners of capital to dictate (through marketing and advertisement) the tastes and thereby the "needs" of the public. Not only is what is represented in the painting at issue, but also the very painting itself. Just as Panini painted the gallery of Cardinal Valenti Gonzaga in the eighteenth century, so did many Flemish and Italian artists typically provide this self-referential image of the value of collecting art, of having private galleries in one's palace, of owning artworks and displaying them to others. The owners of capital, now the owners of art, are in a position to turn their pride possessions into valuable objects that then become desirable to a larger public (let's say the aspiring middle classes). What about the proletariat? Capitalists have a ready-made answer: they can buy the reproductions of original and authentic works only we can own. The age of mechanical reproduction is one of twofold lamentation—not only for the loss of authenticity, but also because of the power of capitalists to dictate the tastes and purchases of the proletariat.

We contend that what determines, classifies, and reifies human creations into artworks is the willingness of people to pay for them and extract them from circulation. In doing so, they are emulating the popes and princes who found aesthetic and transcendental value in artworks regardless of their monetary value. Money was only an instrument to acquire beauty and transform it from a commodity one buys and sells into a sacred and scarce item only one can own. In this sense, then, one can pose the question: isn't art therefore the only site where capitalism is kept at bay? Has the art world in fact set itself apart from the pressures of the marketplace, because of its defiance of the incessant pressure to be bought and sold so as to maintain a "priceless" status? The romantics of the present day would like us to believe that this is still the case.

However, they fail to acknowledge the fact that most Renaissance

54

◇

works were commissioned pieces that fit particular spaces or were executed within architectural designs. As such, they were indeed one of a kind—their ownership could not be transferred without the sale of the entire edifice. The contemporary romantics also fail to account for the changes that have taken place over the past three hundred years in the cultural settings of the exchange of artworks. For example, what was a necessary convenience (creating an illustration of a proposed design for a fresco in order to get the approval of the pope and be paid for the commission) has become bona fide art itself—the drawing or painting. The portable two-dimensional representation rolled and transported from the studio to the palace acquired an artistic status of its own. (Our discussion of the Christos in chapter 4 will return to these themes.)

These objects, once legitimated as artworks in and of themselves, could be more easily traded—bought and sold—by numerous collectors. These collectors were increasingly drawn from the rising middle class of the nineteenth century that wanted to emulate the aristocracy and its appetite for beauty and now had the money to do so. Add to this the role of galleries and art dealers as the brokers of taste and social prestige, and an entire new market was created. (It is interesting to note in this context the extent to which art dealers have become themselves celebrities and gatekeepers of aesthetics, so much so that books are devoted to their success and fame; see Jones and de Coppet.) What precious stones alone may have done in the past, artworks were doing then and continue more openly to do now: legitimating the status of the nouveaux riches.

While Karl Marx describes the dialectical material shift from feudalism to capitalism, the Frankfurt school describes the historical shift from the individuality of oil painting to the art of mechanical reproduction. In their respective ways, they alert us to the gradual process by which originality and authenticity, perhaps even aesthetic transcendence, have been lost. In this sense, then, Walter Benjamin agrees with the lament of the romantics, decrying the loss of art as a means by which to defy the intrusion of capitalism into every facet of life.

Dalia Judovitz's recent critical reassessment of Duchamp's readymades explores the prejudices concerning the value of art as it is carried on into the present. According to Judovitz, "There is, however, something fundamental shared by art and economics: the notion of value. . . . What fascinates Duchamp is the process by which a work acquires artistic and commercial value. The production of value entails, for him, a social and speculative dimension" (162). In this fashion, Judovitz connects

Duchamp's interest in technoscientific innovations and their intimate relation to the world of commerce, so much so that his own creations, his own "productions," are themselves partially commercial and partially artistic. The collapse of these categories, categories whose own value is constantly being challenged, is what characterizes the dawn of the avant garde in the twentieth century.

If we return for a moment to the split between exchange value and aesthetic value, we find that, according to the Frankfurt school, there is no aesthetic value left: it has been co-opted and corrupted. All one can have is artifacts whose beauty is reduced to their price. But this sad state of affairs cannot remain unchanged. The avant-garde is anointed by this viewpoint to overthrow this oppressive market force: it will provide the alternative that is not contaminated by the capitalist system. Avant-garde artists will refuse to think of their work in terms of the prices that they can command in the marketplace, and will inspire the public to transcend their daily material obsessions and envision the kingdom of heaven on earth. Are we back to the popes? More accurately, is it possible to return to the Renaissance—or, for that matter, to the pharaohs?

In the spirit of the detached engagement characterizing our assessment of the avant-gardist relation with technoscience (described in chapter 1), the avant-garde artists may seem to defy their financial surroundings, yet must remain hostage to them like any other workers and artists. To achieve the critical status of avant-garde artist, one must see this predicament and embrace it. One cannot simply say that one does not want to play the capitalist game or the game of the marketplace for artworks. Rather, one must struggle with these games, and as Lyotard says, invent new moves. It is presumptuous to believe one can change the game, or that one has the power to undermine capitalism as such. Yet, an avant-garde artist can demonstrate the limits and fragility of the entire world view within which some work is sanctioned and some is not, some has value and some does not.

For example, it is difficult to ascertain if the judgment one makes about the beauty of a work of art is limited to one's subjective and emotional reaction or is shared by many others. This puzzle can be found in Kant's concern with aesthetic judgments in relation to or by contradistinction from scientific and moral judgments. The notion of the sublime has played an important historical role as a buffer or an excuse not to deal with this puzzle. Once the sublime enters the stage, all judgments are presumed to be objective or at the very least acquire the status of inter-

56 subjectivity (we can all conventionally agree that this is an awe-inspiring
◇ object that affects every individual), and the shift from subjective to
objective judgment seems seamless. The sublime, by definition, is beyond
classification; it stands outside crude material standards. Yet, a society
needs standards by which assessment can be made, whether about art or
about food. This is where the gold standard was introduced so as to reg-
ulate all commodity transactions. Can the gold standard apply in the case
of art?

Kant, the Enlightenment guru, would say no. Even Lyotard, the postmodern rebel, would say no. For them, awe-inspiring works cannot be
reduced to a monetary measure. Though they would agree that the culture defines the meaning and value of the sublime, they would, like the
Frankfurt school, prefer to retain a sanctuary for the sublime outside the
world of commerce. But can they? Even if they can, is their refuge not an
artificial construct for the privileged? Are they creating a Sistine Chapel
of their own? Against this backdrop, it makes sense to speak of the avant-
garde as an interesting attempt to critically engage the marketplace without the belief that one can ever fully escape it, or to collapse some traditional categories and classifications that no longer hold true (high and low
art, commercial and fine art). The detached engagement of the avant-
garde is an acknowledgment of the material trappings of aesthetic value
that cannot be dismissed simply with a heavy dose of idealism.

In this confrontation, the avant-garde artists we choose to examine
here seem to have intentionally discarded their idealistic blinders so as to
acknowledge the predicament described above. And here, once again, we
formulate our view of the role of the avant-garde at the end of the twentieth century and the beginning of the twenty-first. Our concern is not to
set the avant-garde apart from the rest of the art world, but rather to suggest that it is at the very core of this world. The avant-garde is not a movement or a subgroup within the art world that leads the way out of the
bondage of commodity production. Rather, it is a group of individuals who
are highly immersed in the art world's daily interactions with the world of
commerce, and whose distinction is that they are self-conscious of this
immersion and its inescapable predicaments. Both Yves Klein and J. S. G.
Boggs realize the limitation of their own gestures toward the overwhelming power of the marketplace, as avant-garde artists are bound to do. In
realizing their limitations, they seem to have reintroduced a level of
authenticity that is lacking in the romanticized postures of those who

claim that their avant-garde gestures are excluded from the capitalist dominance of everything artistic.

Klein and the Gold Standard

In their artistic works, Yves Klein and J. S. G. Boggs have managed to alert their audiences to the paradoxical relationship that artists have with the world of commerce. Klein, a prominent member of the post–World War II French avant-garde, used gold leaf to surface a group of his paintings ("Monogold" series, 1962) and in a performance work symbolically tossed gold particles into the Seine. These works have immediate reference to the complex history of the use of gold in medieval and Renaissance works commissioned by popes and princes. Klein reminds modern audiences that the temptations of the golden calf remain as strong as ever. Does gold retain its transcendental inferences today? Is the value of art secured by a gold standard? Or does it have its own aesthetic standard? Boggs, as we shall see in the next section, struggles to answer this question in relation to bank notes whose face value is no longer backed by gold. His drawings of dollar bills of various denominations are exchanged for meals at restaurants and for other goods and services. Though deliberate reproductions punishable by law, they have been willingly accepted by merchants and art collectors. In their respective ways (analyzed in more detail below), both Klein and Boggs challenge the implicit assumption that art has a definite value only when it is sold for a price. What, then, is the value of art? Whatever someone is willing to pay for it? Is an exchange the defining moment of valuation?

As we saw earlier in the case of Simmel, to shift from a subjective to an objective valuation of objects requires a certain detachment from those engaged in the exchange. The celebrated marketplace dictates prices in light of the demand for and the supply of objects of desire. But instead of bartering between individuals, instead of being in the awkward position of figuring anew every time a transaction is to take place, a convenient means of exchange has developed. Precious metals secured that means; eventually, their practical replacement became bank notes or paper money. But why would anyone trust a piece of paper or the bank that issues it? Why did the dentist trust Duchamp's check/drawing? Obviously it was because Duchamp was a well-known artist and not a con man—his signature alone was worth a dentist's visit (as Picasso and many other

58 celebrities understood; we'll discuss this further in the next chapter).
◇   These instruments of exchange are representations of a presumed value, and as most countries understood, they must be backed by something that is universally recognized as having a lasting or fixed value—gold! As the Chicago school economist Milton Friedman says: "It [gold] has a long history as a monetary standard; many countries profess to be on a gold standard or to intend to return to or adopt a gold standard. Gold is widely used as a circulating medium, and tens of millions of people all over the world regard gold as 'money,' if not the only 'true' money" (239).

The justification for using gold as opposed to other commodities is grounded historically (it has "emotional appeal," as Friedman concedes) and has some practical appeal: gold is durable and easily divisible. Moreover, to ensure its price level its supply must and can be controllable in terms of mining and storage (bank vaults). The gold standard imposes a certain level of government discipline and control, so that inflationary pressures can be met and diverted, as would be the case, say, in relation to a government's abuse of a budget deficit. What this commodity allows for is a measure of economic success or failure that can be internationally compared. By contrast, if governments refuse to have the gold standard or its equivalent, then they in fact license themselves to print as much currency (paper money) as they wish, and thereby disregard any measure of economic discipline and fiscal control. In developing countries this happens often, and therefore their currency is not traded on the open market; it is considered worthless. There are hard currencies and soft ones—those one will accept and those one will not trade at all. As will become apparent in the next chapter, a similar distinction can be made in the art world: there are objects stored in museums whose value is never threatened, and there are objects circulating in the commercial market whose value is so volatile that they may never be traded again. The economic strength and stability of a country is measured, even today, in relation to its foreign trade, natural resources, gross national product, budget deficit, and gold reserves, and not in relation to its cultural treasures.

The concern with global and national valuation of money does impinge on the art world in two related ways. On the one hand, art is put in its historical precarious position of having its own standard, namely, sublime experience or transcendence—how can one ever expect to buy or sell spirituality? On the other hand, the producers and consumers of art live within a marketplace where commodities, from food and shelter to clothes and luxury items, circulate according to monetary devices. Can the art standard ever compete with the gold standard, that is, be fully recognized internationally as an absolute measure of value? Can the gold standard impose its discipline and limit the inflationary pressure of human tastes and desires, even curtail their fickle changes? Or does the art standard always rely on the gold standard for validation? Does art have value only if someone pays for it in gold?

Klein tries to answer these questions. He acknowledges the economic context within which artworks circulate. In his performance work "Ritual for the Relinquishing of Immaterial Zones of Pictorial Sensibility," Klein proposes an exchange with a prospective buyer on the bank of the Seine River in Paris. He carried out eight of these transfers of an "immaterial substance" during the period from 18 November 1959 to 10 February 1962 (Restany 57). Here is Fineberg's description of what happens in this sale of an "art object": "The buyer met the artist on the quai of the Seine, delivered a prescribed quantity of gold [20 grams], in exchange for 'Immaterial Zones of Pictorial Sensibility' and received a receipt which, following the terms of the agreement, the buyer solemnly burned. The artist then threw half of the gold into the river and the entire transaction was recorded in photographs" (226).

Here is a more detailed account of this event or sale by Thomas McEvilley:

> Beginning in 1959, he [Klein] acted out the establishment of the post-governmental age by the systematic selling of "The Immaterial Zones of Pictorial Sensibility," that is, blocks of the Void— immaterial real-estate of the age of space, paid for in the timeless currency, gold.
>
> Meeting Klein on the bank of the Seine a buyer paid pure gold (a different weight for each zone) to the artist, who then gave him a signed receipt. Then the buyer burned the receipt while Klein threw half the gold into the river. Only then was the Zone permanently relinquished by the Proprietor of Space and transferred to the buyer, who was left with no visible object or documentation except—in some cases—photographs. (46)

Reading these descriptions of Klein's artwork, one is struck by a deeper critical concern than with the standard of exchange and whether the aesthetic standard can ever compete with or replace the gold standard. From our perspective, Klein's critique is a Marxist critique of com-

60

◇

modity exchange. According to Marx, what transforms the barter economy, where one commodity is exchanged for another (C-C) in a never-ending chain of exchange, is the introduction of money, so that money becomes the medium of exchange (C-M-C). Commodities are still exchanged, but money interferes with the direct exchange. Eventually money is accumulated, and then it forms a more crucial link in the chain of exchange (M-C-M), so that a commodity is bought in order to sell it for a profit, namely, more money at the end of the transaction. As time goes on, money instruments are exchanged for money instruments, so that no commodity as such is even part of the chain of exchange (M-M), as happens routinely in financial markets, option exchanges, and bonds and stocks.

Marx decried alienation from nature and eventually from humanity in the transformation of the modern chain of exchange, and Klein seems to echo this lament in his artwork. (Antecedents of this lament have been mentioned already in chapter 1 in conjunction with the views of Duchamp and Magritte.) Klein illustrates how we have lost sight of the fact that every exchange involves a commodity, even when it is amorphous. When he "sells" an "immaterial zone"—air—to a buyer who seems to "buy" nothing, since there is no trace or object that is being tendered, an exchange is still taking place. Even if the receipt as a trace is burned, and even when the gold is cast into the water, there is something that changes hands. And to make sure we realize this point, Klein helps his audience by keeping half of the gold. Klein's gesture acknowledges Marx's concern and thereby also acknowledges the fact that Klein needs the gold to live on, namely, that he must operate within a capitalist system (he never fully escapes the modern chain of exchange). It is interesting to note that the seeming absurdity of commodifying air in Paris in the late 1950s and early 1960s has become a reality in the U.S., where air rights have a value, whether in real estate transactions in New York City or in terms of telecommunication.

The avant-gardist Duchamp had already designated air as a commodity in his work "Air de Paris" (1919). He created for the wealthy American collectors Walter and Louise Arensberg, people who had everything money can buy, a special art object the value of which could not be measured by any standard heretofore used. Duchamp asked a pharmacist to empty one of his medicine containers and then reseal it in Paris. Once resealed, the container held nothing but Parisian air. This container was transformed, by the action of a well-known artist whose works were already collected by the Arensbergs, from a medicine bottle into an art object. As this object was a gift, a token of appreciation, a traded item that would not circulate anymore in the pharmaceutical marketplace, it took on the status of a collectible work of art (D'Harnoncourt and McShine 291). Duchamp's point was simple: only he had the power to sanction any object and turn it into a piece of art; only he could expect the American collectors to grant his gift the status of an art object.

When two passersby along the Seine exchange a smile, what happens? Martin Buber would say that they may have formed, even if for an instant, an "I-Thou" relationship the impact of which may be more profound than many years of interaction. Yet, the exchange of a smile, a gesture, a nod of the head, or a wave of the hand all betray the amorphous character of human exchanges. We exchange something unquantifiable. That is different, of course, from exchanging gifts the value of which can be determined in the marketplace. What about gifts of generosity and goodwill? And what about gifts one makes? Here the nature of one's personality and creativity come into play—art in the making—and now one may wish to appeal to an aesthetic standard as opposed to the gold standard. Klein's exchange of air for gold that is cast away tries to point out that there is a thin line between the fully and partially commodified human world, and that crossing that line is something one cannot avoid.

Klein is an avant-garde artist from our perspective because he admits that artists cannot avoid the commodification of human exchanges. The art standard, if there is such a uniform standard at all, depends on the gold standard for its legitimation power. Without the gold standard in the background, aesthetic value would remain a subjective matter outside the world of human exchange. What makes Klein an interesting avant-garde artist is his critical engagement with the real estate market, his appreciation of the absurdity of buying and selling pieces of land or of water and air and his realization that even when he makes his point, he must be paid for it. He photographs the exchange, using rather than shunning technology (see previous chapter), so that his point can gain the publicity to propel him to celebrity status (see next chapter), and he ends up making money off his critique (just as stock brokers and real estate agents do).

But Klein the critic feels the weight of his own critique and realizes the inevitability of his predicament. His relief painting *The Tomb—Here Lies Space* (1962) portrays the contamination of art with gold. This horizontally displayed, gold-colored canvas has on it a blue wreath, pink (now faded to white) roses, and scattered sheets of gold leaf. (Incidentally,

62   these colors reflect Klein's symbolic triad of universal spiritually.) The
◊   piece is well known from a photograph by Harry Shunk in which Klein's
head peers from one end, as if he were buried underneath this surface—
is it his tomb? What lies "here" is not really "space," that is, a metaphor
of universal spirituality, but rather the artist himself, his idealism. Klein's
lament as a Marxist idealist or humanist is displayed in this piece as that
of someone who cannot escape the gold standard, as hard as he tries.
Klein cannot push aside the tomb door, nor can he be resurrected; the
finality of his situation betrays his acceptance of some, if not all, of the
gold handed to him. Is there room or hope for redemption? Or has the
artist lost the fight against encroaching commercial capitalism?

Klein prays for hope and redemption in his own romantic, quasi-
religious manner. It may be informative to pause here and interlace our
critical evaluation of Klein's art pieces with Pierre Restany's account of
Klein's views concerning the "Blue Revolution," outlined in a letter Klein
wrote President Dwight Eisenhower on 20 May 1958. Klein envisioned a
world order that would be built on the guiding principles of the French
Revolution of 1789, but added another dimension to it: quality (and
thereby sensitivity and responsibility), in addition to liberty, equality, and
fraternity. As far as Restany can piece together, Klein proposed to replace
the modern powers of state capitalism and the political order that sanc-
tions its abuses with an alternative government overseeing powers that
would ensure a more equitable bartering system sensitive to the quality of
the objects exchanged. Restany quotes Klein: "In such a system the rich
man will necessarily be an authentic genius in his specialty. That, in a
word, will be simply justice" (85).

Klein sought to find a middle ground in the split between the gold
and the aesthetic standards—a standard of quality that could be used on
either side of this dividing line. Once quality is monetarily rewarded and
also expresses real aesthetic value, then it is justified (his sense of justice).
Here Klein admits that art does not escape the commercial marketplace,
but rather tries to find a way of legitimating its peculiar pricing mecha-
nism. This, of course, is a utopian proposal.

Restany reports another revealing detail in his account of the ritual
exchanges of gold and air. Half of the gold Klein retained from the "Immaterial Zones" transactions, his so-called profit, was not fully consumed by
him (54). Half of his half was donated at the shrine of his patron saint,
Rita of Cascia, Italy's "patron saint of lost causes" (19). Is Klein under the
spell of Zeno's paradox? This halving process always leaves a residual so

that he will never be left empty-handed. What is left forever is an acknowledgment of the reality of the gold standard of the economy and how it is inexorably linked to the standard of spirituality.

Klein is a rebel who reluctantly accepts the spoils of his culture. He is a critic who knows how to make a buck from the predicament of the art world. He is a financial wizard who makes something out of nothing, intertwining the art world with the world of commerce, while eschewing identification as a sell-out artist. He maintains his integrity in the face of financial temptation by highlighting the power of the golden calf, not by denying its appeal. With this detached and engaged attitude, then, Klein is an avant-gardist.

This designation of Klein would be accepted by Poggioli, who argues about the transformation of the working conditions of artists in the twentieth century: they lose the status of craftsmen and become "self-employed professional provider[s] of services." Once the artist is cast in the precarious position of a worker whose product is a service and not an object of consumption, once his works are subject to the pressures of the bourgeois marketplace, and once he loses the tradition of economic dependency on a prefigured patronage, "the roads to economic fortunes are open to the modern artist to an extent wholly unthinkable in earlier societies." On the other hand, the artist, "when he lets himself be tempted, can only count on chance and luck since the public he might want to address cannot be reduced to a definite entity" (113–14). Is Klein just "lucky," or is he an alienated radical whose ambivalence about capitalism can be expressed only through a direct deployment of the exchange of gold?

Boggs: Forging the Art of Money

The gold bullion of the gold standard cannot be confused with the gold leaf on a piece of art. When Klein uses gold in his pieces no one can accuse him of stealing it from its legitimate owners (he buys gold for his works). When Klein uses gold he in fact uses a commodity, and not its instrument of exchange. That, however, is not the case with bank notes. Notes, checks, and currency bills have no commodity value in and of themselves—their only value is their power of exchange. The exception is the value of notes when they become rare, when they are taken out of circulation. Perhaps then one can appreciate their aesthetic value.

Once again, we are faced with the predicament of what is and what

64 is not a piece of art—what constitutes a means of exchange in contradis-
◊ tinction to a collectible object on display in a home or a museum. Enter
J. S. G. Boggs, contemporary American artist, who was headquartered in
the United Kingdom and now works in Pittsburgh. His artwork is also a
critique of the commercialization of the art world, as well as of the necessity of commodity circulation and its subsequent valuation. But unlike
numerous artists who preceded him (Ray Johnson, for example, who in
1970 did a series of collages that incorporated dollar bills), Boggs is not
satisfied with simply handing over a piece of art, a sketch, to a restaurant
proprietor as a form of payment (as Picasso and Matisse did). This transaction is still sanctioned by commodity circulation; it only hints at the loss
of the barter system. The proprietor knows full well that there is a value
to the piece beyond its aesthetic value—it can be sold on the open market. How can one defy this inevitable situation?

Klein questions the perceived value of commodities (selling nothing-
ness); Boggs questions the perceived value of money (producing it). Here
we are focusing only on some of Boggs's works with money images. In
meticulous drawings that render bank notes of various nations in correct
dimensions, and with uncannily accurate detail, Boggs creates by hand
his own notes as a de facto replacement for those issued by central governments and, in the U.S., the Federal Reserve. They remain obviously
drawings, since his depiction is of only one side (eventually he decides to
reproduce them on two sides). What does Boggs say about his pieces?

In a long interview with Lawrence Weschler in the *New Yorker*, Boggs
makes sure to explain that "the actual drawings of his various bills should
be considered merely small parts—the catalysts, as it were—of his true
art, which consists of the transactions that they provoke" (34). In this
respect, then, he follows Klein's observations about transactions, the
exchange of commodities and money instruments, gold and bank notes.
Unlike Klein, though, he makes the transaction itself a work of art, an
object that is later bought by collectors. While Klein tries to leave no trace
of the actual exchange, requiring the receipt to be destroyed (permitting
only a photographic record of the action), Boggs focuses on the docu-
mentation of the exchange. Here is how it works.

Boggs draws one side (the face) of a bill and then tries to acquire art
supplies or a meal at a restaurant. When the check arrives he tries to con-
vince the waiter or waitress to accept his hand-drawn bill for its face value
as if it were actual money. If the waiter or clerk accepts the drawing,
Boggs makes sure to collect some change and keeps it and the receipt for

his purchase. Then he keeps the transaction secret for twenty-four hours—a cooling-off period, as it were, perhaps in order not to open the transaction for immediate purchase by art dealers and collectors. Then he contacts collectors and art dealers and announces that the transaction took place. At this point an interested party can trace the "owner" of Boggs's piece and try to buy it; if needed, Boggs offers his services for a fee to help find the owner. If the owner of the drawing is willing to sell it, then the collector needs also to buy the receipt and the change from Boggs, and only then has the art object been bought. Obviously, the entire transaction costs more than the face value of the drawing or the change and receipt that accompany it (in most cases ten to twenty times the face value of the drawing).

Boggs follows several rules. His first rule is that he will not "sell" a drawing as an object of art. Instead, his creation must be accepted for its face value in a transaction with another commodity (such as a meal). That is, he will not accept money for his drawing in the sense of an exchange as art. The second rule is that his drawing has to be spent for its face value, thereby becoming a full participant in the chain of exchange (at the gold standard value). His third rule is that his transaction must remain private for one day, so that the art world (collectors, agents, and curators) is kept at bay. His fourth rule deals with what happens after the transaction takes place—he will sell the receipt to an interested party and assist that party (for a fee) in tracing the "owner" of the work so that he or she then can negotiate the full purchase of the transaction.

What is at issue for Boggs? What makes him a candidate for avant-garde status from our perspective? While Weschler focuses primarily on the questions of value and counterfeit, we wish to focus on three related issues that highlight Boggs's critique of the hegemony of the commercialization of art. First, what is at stake in the questioning of money and its purchase power is the *faith* we have in a piece of paper and what it represents. Second, the meticulous drawing of bank notes turns our attention to the *aesthetic value* that money has. And third, the insistence on a prolonged process of exchange, turning one transaction into another, reminds collectors of their *role* in the process of commodity exchange.

Let us examine each point separately. First, the question of faith. There is an implicit separation between religion and commerce in the sense that everything religious is bound by a faith in God and in the spiritual power of the churches that serve His ideals, whereas everything commercial is reducible to dollars and cents. Boggs noticed that the phrase "In

66
◇
God We Trust" on U.S. bills appeared only in the 1930s, once the full backing of gold ceased to be the standard. As Boggs says: "When you could no longer trust in gold, they invited you to trust in God" (Weschler 36). Religious trust is imported into the secular world of commerce when the commercial standards are no longer used. There is no risk in trusting that the bill you carry with you is exchangeable for an ounce of gold, but there is a great risk if all that backs your bill is a trust in God. So, is our entire monetary system built on trust? Must we have faith in our currency, because there is nothing more substantial that backs it?

Using his art, his drawings, Boggs redirects our attention to the value we assume the currency has. He forces us to appreciate that in U.S. currency, bills of the same size may have different numbers printed on their faces, and that it must take a great deal of faith to accept one as worth, say, one hundred dollars, while another of the same size is worth only one dollar. (In many countries the size of the bill changes with its face value.) If the currency we use is worth only what we believe it is worth, why is that not the case with works of art, or, for that matter, with everything else? Here Boggs brings his insights into the precarious status of artworks as valued objects into the very means of exchange, bank notes. The conventions that surround the valuation of art—who is in vogue today and whose works sell well—are also the conventions that surround the valuation of money—who determines and agrees that these green notes are worth that many dollars. Once Boggs turns to reproducing by hand the images of bank notes, he realizes that they also have an aesthetic quality.

The second issue raised by Boggs is the valorization of bank notes for their aesthetic value. For him: "money is more beautiful and highly developed and aesthetically satisfying than the print works of all but a few modern artists. And a dollar bill *is* a print; it's unique, numbered edition" (ibid.). Boggs is less concerned with the mechanical reproduction of dollar bills (an issue that resurfaces when the question of counterfeiting comes up) than with their intricate designs and the careful drawing and symbolic expressions that they display. Boggs suggests that we look at bills of all countries as cultural artifacts that express the prejudices and long-held beliefs of the cultures that use them. As far as he is concerned, one can observe and read these bills as if they had the status of drawings and prints displayed in a museum or gallery.

What takes place in the exchange of money for art is an exchange of one commodity with another. This observation pushes the clock back from hypercapitalism to feudalism, from the exchange of one money instrument with another to the exchange of one commodity of aesthetic value with another of equal aesthetic value. Incidentally, this is a romanticized view of monetary instruments, because it refuses to accept money instruments as neutral objects without value in and of themselves: they, too, have a status worth preserving. (One could make a similar argument about shares issued by corporations or bonds issued by local and federal governments.) When Boggs copies bank notes he in fact pays homage to their beauty, just as students and apprentices copy the paintings and drawings of old masters. But can Boggs indeed divert the public's attention from dismissing bills as the means for exchange to appreciating their own value?

Here we arrive at the third point we appreciate about Boggs's avant-gardism. It is in fact the public that Boggs tries to reach, rather than the elite group of art dealers, museum and gallery curators, and private collectors. The transactions that Boggs stages involve at the beginning clerks and wait staffs, not art dealers and collectors (who may be added later). He approaches those least concerned with so-called high culture, perhaps also the least aware of the aesthetic values and the cultural critiques that accompany it. He wants to cajole them, the less educated, less sophisticated traders in the marketplace, to accept his drawings as if they were worth something. They (the wait staff and clerks) don't know who he is; they don't know the value of his drawings. To them, he is just another con man trying to get a free meal or film or art supplies in exchange for a little drawing that he produces out of his satchel. His drawing does not have the immediate, tangible value that a twenty-dollar bill has; they have to take a risk, put their own money in the till, and walk away with a drawing. Can they pay their rent with it? Probably not.

But if he can initiate them, the aesthetically and culturally unsophisticated (in terms of high art), into his profound critique of commercial transactions, if he can break down and challenge their implicit assumptions about value and money, perhaps he can explain what drives him to do what he does. If they understand him, more so than if the art dealers and critics do, then he has accomplished something important in his romantic lament over the loss of aesthetic value in the midst of capitalist reproduction. Only when they have accepted him, have agreed to have faith in his drawing, have demonstrated by their action and the risk they take that his drawing is worth at least as much as a bank note, have elevated his work to exchangeable commodity—only then he will let those who wish to profit from his challenge enter the chain of transactions. He

68 forces the art dealers to deal with people they never have to negotiate
◇   with, treating them as if they were themselves collectors, since they have
inadvertently become the owners of a collectible work of art. Once again,
Boggs disrupts the neat chain of transaction that has become common in
the art world; once again, he forces us to think about the activities we take
for granted and those we must undertake in order to distinguish the world
of commerce from the art world.

According to the art critic Arthur Danto, what is at stake for Boggs
and his interlocutors is the game of chance they are induced into playing:
"And the superlatively drawn note exits initially to precipitate a complex
happening in which the 'Viewer' is induced to play a role and run a risk.
Boggs' is a postmodern art form, a mode of interaction between audience
and artist in which each takes chances which go considerably beyond the
traditional concept, central to the ideals of painting since ancient times,
of cognitive error, of taking painted grapes for real fruit" (1994, 106). What
exactly is the risk at hand? Is it that of counterfeit? Not quite, since Boggs
makes it clear all along that he is drawing paper money. Rather, the risk,
as far as Danto is concerned, is twofold: "It exposes Boggs to real risks just
because the government holds a monopoly on the issuance of currency,
and Boggs, in getting the Viewer to participate in the transaction by
accepting the drawing as money, immediately criminalizes the action"
(ibid. 109).

But why would the audience be more willing nowadays to take the
risk in the very activity of viewing the art, and then be induced to
exchange it or eventually "buy" it? Is this situation tenable because of the
human characteristics already detected in the biblical story of the golden
calf? Danto claims that part of what is at stake for a wider audience is the
appreciation of the art world in general and of its financial undertones in
particular. Danto says: "The public is now more aware of the art market,
and is more conscious of the potential increase or decrease in the value
of any work of art. Boggs counts on that consciousness, thereby keeping
the Viewer-Participant-Owner engaged" (ibid. 108).

Yet, one could take Danto's assessment to task for being insensitive to
related issues that arise when money and its representation become the
focus of attention. What about a neo-Marxian critique (perhaps but not
necessarily along John Berger's lines) that problematizes the ability to
appreciate an aesthetic aspect of money? Isn't money a means to survival
for most people? While claiming that Boggs enhances an aesthetic appreciation of money and of art, Danto fails to acknowledge that most people

he targets (wait staff, for instance) do not have the luxury of parting with their hard-earned money in order to "collect" it. For them, there is a much greater risk of failing to pay their rent or utility bills for the sake of raising their aesthetic consciousness, in Danto's sense.

We claim that Boggs is still a committed artist, just as Klein is, despite accepting both as avant-gardists. Our claim is based on the appeal Boggs makes to an aesthetic standard (and value) that should transcend that of the marketplace. Both Klein and Boggs want to challenge the gold standard and the decisions that revolve around it because they want to rescue and uphold the value of art for art's sake, the value of having an aesthetic experience, of being awed. Yet, they recognize that such an experience must be interlaced with some aspects of the world of commerce, whether money or gold. They both try to mock contemporary collectors and humiliate them publicly, whether by making them chase their works or by giving them "nothing" in exchange for their money or gold. Perhaps they want to remind them that they are neither popes nor princes, but merchants chasing a buck for a profit. Perhaps they want to illustrate how difficult it is to bring about spiritual transcendence in the midst of capitalist culture. Or perhaps they want to position themselves as saints and saviors, as the only ones who transcend the reduction of art to money, while quietly accepting "real money" and "real goods" with which to make a living and promote their art and themselves.

The Inevitability of Commercial Exchange

Renaissance artists understood that in order to elevate their work and their compensation from the lows of craftsmanship to the highs of artistry, they had to deal with the elite of their culture, popes and princes. They also understood that they had to sell their art, figuratively and literally. Works of art became unique and even collectible, and the signature of the individual artist was essential in order to procure the appropriate compensation. Apprentices and assistants were routinely employed because of the magnitude of the projects, but the genius of Michelangelo and Raphael could not be simply reproduced by anyone. Once art no longer plays the role of an added service to the construction of palaces and temples, or the role of a religious appeal for spiritual transcendence, it must play new roles—and so it did by the twentieth century.

We alluded earlier that, according to both Simmel and Berger in different contexts, art reflects the social and economic status of its own-

70
◇

ers. That is, the power to purchase a luxury item that has no use value whatsoever (except for satiating aesthetic appetites) illustrates excess wealth. The display of artworks on one's wall can be seen as denoting the window into the vaults in which great wealth is accumulated and stored. It is no accident that among the first impressionist paintings sold in the U.S. in the 1870s was Degas's *Cotton Exchange in New Orleans* (1873). The content of the painting showed clearly what was culturally important and what someone would be interested in petrifying on one's walls—the commercial life of the culture. As we noted in the previous chapter, Duchamp and Magritte in their own ways set the tone for other artists of the twentieth century: art cannot survive outside the world of commerce.

Although the art world and the world of commerce have historically and theoretically been kept separate (because of the pretensions that the former has only aesthetic value and the latter only exchange value), it becomes evident that this has not really been the case. The question then becomes, what relationship do these two worlds have? Do they overlap? Is one engulfed by the other? Raising these questions and providing alternative answers has been left to philosophers and art critics. But as far as we are concerned, these questions are most ingeniously raised and answered by avant-garde artists who are self-conscious of the activity in which they are engaged, and who realize that they do not work in a vacuum. The culture that surrounds them confines their imagination and limits their activities; it legitimates their work and licenses them to continue. In this sense, then, they are also products of the culture they help produce.

Klein and Boggs ask two related questions: what makes an object an art object, and what role does money play in the transactions undertaken by artists and collectors alike? Whether they gesture to the air or to bank notes, they force us to recall Duchamp's focus on mechanical objects, such as a bicycle wheel and a propeller, and Magritte's bottle labels and advertising posters. In all of these cases, these artists push the limits of the art world and force the public to find aesthetic value in the world of commerce. Boggs's obsession with the beauty of the print-work in a bank note is only an extension of the general rebellion against the confines of the museum and the collector's palace. As far as they are concerned, beauty can be found everywhere, if one stops to appreciate it.

If one were to follow Benjamin's critique and bemoan the loss of aesthetic value in the age of mechanical reproduction, itself an exhibition of romanticized lament reminiscent of religious purity and spiritual zeal,

Boggs will interrupt this line of thought with his insistence that even reproductions (such money bills) are unique insofar as they have individual serial numbers. As we shall see in the next chapter, Andy Warhol pushes this theme to another extreme by reproducing images on large canvases, displaying the beauty one can find in everyday objects such as soup cans and soda bottles. The iconography that fascinates the artists discussed in the next chapter differs from religious iconography only in degree and not in kind. Twentieth-century culture worships commercialism and the exchange of commodities of all kinds, with a material craving that seems in principle to be insatiable. What religious fervor was in the Middle Ages so is material possession in the modern world.

What baffles us as we review this aspect of the art world is how few of the artists are open about this transformation of the art world into the world of commerce. Instead of decrying the loss of aesthetic appeal and the purity of the art world, pretending to be critical but remaining romantic religionists, we would recommend the prescription of some of the avant-gardists: acknowledge the predicament, embrace its thorny crown, carry its cross, and undermine its ugly underbelly whenever you can. Don't pretend to be able to escape the world of commerce, but turn it on itself, show its beauty, and force its participants to be more self-conscious of what they implicitly endorse. These statements and pronouncements require an appreciation of the capitalist system and its elasticity.

Unlike Marx's critique of capitalism, we don't believe that it is crisis prone and will eventually self-destruct. Rather, we believe that capitalism is a postmodern system that accommodates its historical antecedents with new innovations, being able to reduce labor tension and class struggle by providing ownership of the modes of production almost to every worker through pension funds and the stock market. We mention these issues only as a backdrop against which to appreciate the sophistication of some of the avant-garde artists we mention in this book. We see them as pioneers bridging the presumed gaps between the worlds of art and commerce. If they succeed, they publicize their stunts against the system but do so within the system—they end up celebrities and wealthy artists! Their critique is heard because it is immanent to the system, and it itself is commodified and enters the marketplace.

The marketplace has expanded over the past century and engulfed everything in its way: from religious piety to honor and trust. One endows a chair at Harvard, a sanctuary at a church, or a cabinet position—it all depends how much it costs. With proper patronage one can become a

72

◇

celebrity even if one lacks the means to buy one's way to the top. Now that art no longer is acquired by a small number of privileged leaders, it enters the arena of public exchange and debate. We have galleries and museums in every city and town, and every home is adorned by some form of art. The proliferation of art and its various reproductions has made the questions we ask more visible and more urgent than they were before. The art market, more specifically, has expanded as well, and now is treated as if it were another market where commodities are exchanged. When the stock market in the U.S. is booming and millions are made overnight, the art market expands as well and millions of dollars are spent on buying artworks. In fact, as Richard Rush outlines, the art market at times surpasses the stock market in the increase of value of the commodities that it incorporates. The art market also drops less during a depression than the stock market, perhaps because the very wealthy are less inclined to dump their collections at any price the market will bear. For them the aesthetic standard cannot be compromised; the art standard becomes more stable than the gold standard (385).

Rush's analysis of the commercial value of art and the market conditions under which it operates focuses on the art market in the Western Hemisphere, the United States, and western Europe (Japan is a latecomer to this market), where one finds the largest number of art transactions (and the development of auction houses in addition to galleries and art dealers). According to Rush, as of 1960 roughly five hundred individuals comprised the entire "market for high priced works of art" (besides the institutional buyers). High prices at the time meant more than $50,000 per item, and as such allowed a narrow range of participation by only the very wealthy. This small group, combined with what Rush calls "high salaried people," accounted for the bulk (75 percent) of the typical gallery purchases of items more moderately priced. Rush demonstrates the concentration of market control by a minute percentage of those who appreciate beauty in art (352–53). His survey brings to mind the Marxian concern over the concentration of capital (the ownership of the means of production) by fewer and fewer individuals.

But, as Ulrike Klein reminds us, "The art market is a *communication market* rather than a commodity market. Almost every dealer considered *communication* the most valuable resource in the quest for information about art and the art world" (22). Klein goes on to explain that the relationship among art dealers, gallery owners, museum curators, private collectors, and the artists themselves depends on more than the "quality" of the work. The work, as well as the artist, must be marketable, must appeal to potential buyers: "An art work must elicit from the recipient an emotional as well as an intellectual response and challenge his or her thinking process through *imagination* and *innovation*. The work should carry the stamp of the specific artist, distinguishing it from the work of any other artist. And last but not least, the quality of an art work will also be judged by the professionalism of the craft—the work should be 'rather well done'" (2–3).

Even when the work is well done, argue some gallery directors and owners, the pricing of artworks remains elusive. Does the work have decorative value only (that is, does it fit into the interior design of a home), or does it also have an art value that depends on the history of the artist and the sales of such works over a long period of time (Klein 6–13)? Gallery owners representing artists for the first time have to launch advertising campaigns that include private openings, fancy parties, and media hype, in order to execute the first transaction. (These strategies are central to the promotion of aesthetic value, as will be seen in the next two chapters in conjunction with Warhol, Haring, and the Christos.) They have obstacles similar to those encountered by Boggs when he tries to "sell" his money drawings for the first time.

One of the advantages that art dealers and collectors have is their ability to appeal to the celebrity status of both the artists and the owners of their works. Art works supersede their so-called original intent (of having aesthetic value, of appealing to one's emotional and spiritual sensibilities, of providing the means for transcendence) and become trade objects—they add their particular twist to the ever growing commodification of life as if it were a question of survival. If art were to circulate only among five hundred collectors, as Rush contends was the case by 1960, then it would become an extinct species. To ensure its survival, the art world had to accommodate itself to the realities of the marketplace: it had to be more openly commercial. Just as half of the business section of every daily newspaper lists the prices of commodities, stocks, and bonds, so there is a regular reporting of the changing prices of artworks. Art objects have become private investments, as opposed to being priceless objects of lasting admiration in the public domain.

Yves Klein and J. S. G. Boggs stripped bare the art standard and the pretense of beauty as an experience no money can buy, and have made clear how much the art world is held hostage to the strictures of commodity exchange. Whether or not artists are willing hostages remains an open

74
◇
question, as the next chapter will show. If artists are willing participants in the world of artistic commerce, then they become less interesting for our purposes. What we focus on is the ambivalent position and the struggle avant-garde artists undertake in order to preserve that which cannot be preserved: artistic purity and an appeal to aesthetic value as a religious calling.

Moreover, the ideal of freedom for artistic creation, the ideal of the free artist pursuing an aesthetic calling, remains bound by the conditions of the marketplace. As Thierry de Duve explains: "Yes, artists are free: they are free to exchange and exchange whatever, but only there where exchange takes place, in the market. They are also free to do whatever, but the violence of this freedom is no longer that of revolution, it is merely that of economic competition." De Duve goes on to explain that to some extent there is nothing new about the pressure of economic conditions or of the market: "The law of the market is not new. It has been there ever since the art market came into being. Even before Courbet it set the economic conditions of modernism and fixed the social condition of the modern artist as a 'free worker' or small entrepreneur. It is only with late modernism, that of Warhol for instance, that the economic conditions of art practice, understood until then to be contingent and external to art properly speaking, became its subject, its substance, and its form" (350).

Warhol, as seen in the next chapter, transposes Klein's and Boggs's concerns and laments, their critiques and works, to a new level of self-awareness that a wider audience can appreciate. This transposition goes beyond competition in the marketplace and beyond opportunism: it is a deeply felt critique of modernity's mechanical reproduction.

3

Private and "Public" Art:
Selling Out?

In the future, we can expect every artist to be a machine
producing poster canvases every fifteen minutes.

—Cicotello and Sassower, with apologies to Andy Warhol

Introduction

IN CHAPTER 1, we noted that Duchamp's ready-mades were conceived
and displayed to highlight the aesthetic quality one could find in manufactured objects. The context of display, the context of consumption, so
to speak, could allow the public gaze to appreciate a urinal, for example,
in a fashion radically different from its function in a public restroom. But
once this statement has been made, what social and cultural consequences reverberate? What is the residue that eventually gets canonized
into art history and the tradition of the avant-garde? What is the aesthetic
and social meaning of Sherrie Levine's creation of a golden urinal—her
fabricated golden calf, titled *After Duchamp*—in 1991, nearly eighty years
after the "original"? Is this mockery (of whom?) run amok, or is it the
enshrining of a cultural symbol whose power of suggestion carries to the
end of the century?

According to John Cage, the reissuing of Duchamp's ready-mades at
the end of his career for sale to the broadest possible public was unacceptable, and he asked, "why did you permit that, because it looks like
business rather than art?" (Judovitz 161). But isn't this precisely the point
under consideration here, namely, that critically engaged avant-garde art
always must be simultaneously like business and like technoscience and
like art? Isn't it the spillover effect of the products of the artistic community into the larger community of consumers? Even Donald Kuspit, who
is always in search of the therapeutic moment of avant-garde art, agrees

76

◇

to view Duchamp's work in this way: "The ready-made, for example, is at once a withdrawal from the object by its presentation as art, and a withdrawal from art by its conception as readymade and found (rather than handmade and created)" (33).

This view is in agreement with what was illustrated in chapter 2, that there is no art outside the commercialized marketplace, there is no art that isn't sold in one form or another. Whether one stretches the sales value of air, as Yves Klein did, or pushes the acceptable limits of exchange value, as J. S. G. Boggs did with his drawings of money, what is foregrounded is the financial context within which art survives. The only "private" moment of art is perhaps the moment of realization by the artist that there are motivating factors that propel her or him to be an artist. So, rather than focus on the aesthetic experience of individual audiences, an experience we would claim is always culturally determined (appreciating beauty is a social construct and not a divine revelation), let us follow a brief classification of motivating factors for artists as producers of commodities whose consumption in the public arena determines their "value."

It may be useful to apply Paula Stephan and Sharon Levin's view of the motivating factors that underlie the scientific community to our concern with the artistic community. According to Stephan and Levin, scientists have three reasons for doing their works: curiosity or puzzle-solving, recognition, and monetary rewards. The first, puzzle-solving or curiosity, emerges as an important but not the single most important motivation for scientific research. There are those who are drawn into a field of research because of their interest in figuring out a problem that has remained unsolved. Similarly, one could argue that some artists are drawn into their chosen field because they are tempted to transform it by bringing to it innovative materials or figuring out how to represent their subjects in a more creative fashion than their predecessors or their contemporaries.

Stephan and Levin's second reason for the motivation of scientists is recognition. Here they are informed by the works of sociologists of science who trace referencing and citation as crucial elements in the political interaction among scientists in their respective institutions. They extend this motivating factor to be psychological and true for all humans, obviously including artists. Recognition is a twofold affair: one needs recognition from within the artistic community, that is, other artists and the institutions of art (schools, museums, galleries, and art history), and from the public (audiences and collectors). Focusing on one would almost

guarantee the other's acceptance at some point, as far as artists are concerned.

The third motivating factor is monetary rewards, and here scientists, whose esoteric activity may seem removed from earthy concerns, turn out to be mini-capitalists. Stephan and Levin quote Stephen Jay Gould, the leading American paleontologist, who says scientists all want "status, wealth, and power, like everyone else" (22). Being like everyone else is neither a condemnation nor a concession. It is simply a realization that within the capitalist context of commercialized technoscience, it would be foolish not to have the material rewards money can buy. Can artists afford to exclude themselves from the world they inhabit? Don't artists need financial rewards for the very production of their work, since they may be less fortunate in being subsidized by teaching or research institutions?

In asking these rhetorical questions, we keep in mind another model or view of avant-garde artists we have learned to reject. It is a view expressed most eloquently by Eugène Ionesco, who says: "An avant-garde man is like an enemy inside the city he is bent on destroying, against which he rebels; for like any system of government, an established form of expression is also a form of oppression. The avant-garde man is the opponent of an existing system" (40–41). Ionesco's view may fit the nineteenth-century view of the historical mission of the avant-garde, but it cannot be sustained during the present day. This is not because of the increased commercialization of the twentieth century, nor is it because technoscience has become commercialized as well. Rather, this is the case because the avant-garde artist and the politician alike have learned that playing the role of an "enemy" yields worse results than playing the role of an anti-elitist leader (in Calinescu's sense). The effectiveness of leadership from within—a critical leadership determined not to destroy the city but to revamp it, an engaged leadership committed to changing the rules of the game in Lyotard's sense (62) and all along being responsible for its complicity—is what makes the avant-garde as we view it more interesting and enigmatic. It's interesting because it can bring about change without destroying the foundations of the past, and enigmatic because its call for change is limited by the traditional trajectory it tries to transform.

Avant-garde artists, therefore, are motivated in a fashion no different from other self-proclaimed leaders of a culture. They also are bound by the realization that they operate within the technoscientific community.

78
◇

Once they are understood to be no different from other professionals who embrace and recoil from the strictures of commercialized technoscience in modern times, our discussion of the role of avant-garde artists in relation to the public and private domains of the production, distribution, and consumption of works of art may seem less awkward. One could also translate the examination of commercial and institutionalized art into this context, and thereby appreciate the blurring of their distinction.

One of the most striking and least apologetic expressions of the intimate relationship between art and business has been made by Andy Warhol: "Business art is the step that comes after Art. I started as a commercial artist, and I want to finish as a business artist. After I did the thing called 'art' or whatever it's called, I went into business art. I wanted to be an Art Businessman or a Business Artist. Being good in business is the most fascinating kind of art. . . . making money is art and working is art and good business is the best art" (1975, 92). Not only is Warhol unapologetic about his fascination with business art, but like Boggs he elevates the means and process by which money exchanges hands and is accumulated into an art form. There is nothing bad or ugly about money; money isn't dirty—it's aesthetically pleasing, as Boggs reminds us; and the business world isn't bad either—it, too, is aesthetically pleasing. As Oskar Bätschmann observes: "Warhol was not criticizing the nature of consumer goods [in the Marxist sense], he was outbidding it by making the goods absolute" (211). Like Magritte before him, Warhol reproduces images of consumer goods; but unlike him, Warhol carries his fascination and exaltation one step further and popularizes and legitimizes Magritte's enigmatic representations of daily consumption.

It should be clear that our focus in this chapter on Andy Warhol and Keith Haring and on what makes their works culturally and aesthetically significant is their interest in—their almost obsession with—making their works accessible to a public beyond the elitist connoisseurs of avant-garde art. Accessibility need not be a mark of commercial sellout or lack of artistic creativity, as some art critics would argue in defending their self-appointed role as mediators and translators. Accessibility need not be an abdication of the critical dimension associated with avant-garde art or a stooping-down to the lowest common denominator of a culture. Instead, accessibility, whether through the image of a urinal or a bicycle or images of cultural icons or consumer goods such as soup cans, becomes a hallmark of ingenuity, critical engagement, and ambivalent acceptance of commercialized technoscience. This view is supported by Matei Calinescu, who notes the historical transformation of the metaphor and lived

reality of the avant-garde from its original incarnations into the late twentieth century. In his words: "The avant-garde, whose limited popularity
had long rested exclusively on scandal, all of a sudden became one of the
major cultural myths of the 1950s and the 1960s. Its offensive, insulting
rhetoric came to be regarded as merely amusing, and its apocalyptic out-
cries were changed into comfortable and innocuous clichés." The avant-
garde is no longer Ionesco's rebel or enemy, but rather the court jester
who carefully reads the culture and delivers the kind of relief one expects
in Shakespeare's plays. Calinescu saves the most powerful assessment for
last: "Ironically, the avant-garde found itself failing through a stupendous,
involuntary success" (121). Accordingly, both the role and definition of the
avant-garde had to be reassessed.

If the success of the avant-garde also signals its demise, as Calinescu
suggests (in agreement with Berman, 50), this means that the avant-garde
was never supposed to be successful. It was expected to remain rebellious,
utopian, and prophetic—outside the mainstream. Yet, this model does not
fit the dissemination of ideas and concerns in the postmodern information age. Biblical prophets had to escape to the desert, but their contemporary incarnations are scientists and artists whose prophecies and judgments are lionized and revered (even when contested)—they even get paid
well to say what they say and do what they do. It may seem unacceptable
to some critics, but the emancipatory potential of the avant-garde is
enhanced rather than diminished by its popular appeal. This is what turns
the idealized elitism of modernity and postmodernity into the material
forces of transformation.

One could argue that accessibility follows one of the strands of Walter Benjamin's ambivalence with the role of technological innovations in
regard to aesthetic experiences. On the one hand, Benjamin bemoans the
loss of authenticity in the age of mechanical reproduction. On the other
hand, in his analysis of film, he admits that such innovations may have an
emancipatory force. As Fredric Jameson explains: "A progressive work of
art is one which utilizes the most advanced artistic techniques, one in
which, therefore, the artist lives his activity as a technician, and through
this technical work find a unity of purpose with the industrial worker"
(81).

So, accessibility within this Marxist model means an alliance between
two sorts of workers, the industrial and the artistic, noticing their engagement with the forces of commercialized technoscience. This kind of
alliance is typical of late nineteenth- and early twentieth-century avant-
garde art. For instance, Brancusi's gleaming, polished-bronze "Bird-in-

80 Space" sculptures of 1923–40 remind one of the aesthetic beauty and
◇ technical challenges of propellers manufactured for use on ships and airplanes. They may not be as powerful messages for their audience as the
movies, but they still relate one's daily experience to one's aesthetic sensibility. They instill a sense of transcendence of time and mobility in space
that overcomes human limitations. The movies, obviously, are more overwhelmingly powerful, as Warhol is quick to say: "It's the movies that have
really been running things in America ever since they were invented. They
show you what to do, how to do it, when to do it, how to feel about it, and
how to *look* how you feel about it" (1985, 11).

To this extent, then, Warhol continues a Marxist tradition of critique
without acknowledging it as such. Perhaps it is because he uses a different vocabulary (than the classical terms of the fetish of commodification);
perhaps the references escape him (Marx's *Capital*); perhaps he wishes to
avoid being associated with (New York, Greenwich Village) Marxist circles. Be that as it may, Warhol is no different from many other artists of
the twentieth century who realize the material implications of the industrial revolution and attempt to work with and not against them, even
when the intent is critical through and through. In this sense, this chapter continues the themes already mentioned in chapter 1 in relation to
technoscience with regard to the works of Duchamp and Magritte.

Warhol's Commercialized Art

Although Warhol and Keith Haring worked in the mid to late twentieth century, they represent the spirit of their predecessors and deliberately
continue the tradition of defiance associated with the avant-garde. They
do so in bringing to the fore the entangled ambiguity of the late nineteenth-century infatuation with and condemnation of the industrial revolution. Their works express a critique of positivist values and fascination
attached to the fruits of science and technology, while simultaneously dis-
tilling moments of awe and the sublime that accompany them (not unlike
the works of Duchamp, Magritte, and the many other avant-garde artists
of the dawn of the twentieth century). They expand and promote blurring
the distinction between fine and popular art and call attention to the role
of artists as celebrities, all the while maintaining the uncomfortable tension between the commercialization of the art world and the critical aspirations of cultural prophets. Kuspit is correct when he notes disapprov-
ingly the celebrity status acquired by some avant-garde artists: "the art of

both Picasso and Duchamp takes us back to the artist, indeed seems to
make him legendary. He, not his art, makes the ultimate claim on our
attention. His life and his art seamlessly fuse, which may be the ultimate
grandiosity" (36).

Yet, the fact that some avant-garde artists have turned their own lives
into works of art, offered themselves on the altar of aesthetic experience
and pursued the quest for a detached engagement with the world of commercialized technoscience, turns them into significant contributors to
their culture. They do not hide behind the institutional walls of their community, but open the gates, letting the public observe and assess, consume and digest.

Perfecting Benjamin's image of mechanical reproductions and stress-
ing Herbert Marcuse's one-dimensionality of human existence within
commercialized consumer society, Warhol fits this description. He takes
a publicity photo of Marilyn Monroe and replicates it on large canvases as
if to flatten her iconographic value into poster- or billboard-size advertisements that the public can confront and enjoy. Similarly, he transforms
the most mundane of commercial art's creations, the labels of Campbell's
canned soups and Brillo boxes, into a legitimate art form for art connoisseurs and museum audiences. Warhol cultivated his celebrity status during his life; Haring gained that status briefly before his premature death.
In his dazzling, colorful, and cartoonlike images, Haring proved that the
entertainment value of art need not undermine its beauty nor compromise its sociopolitical or moral integrity. The playfulness displayed in both
artists' works and personalities does not detract from their convictions
and the seriousness of their message. It reflects the strategy of the court
jester whose engagement cannot be detached.

We have suggested in the last two chapters that in order to appreciate the ambivalence displayed in the art world, one should observe the
detached engagement of artists, that is, their self-conscious and deliberate attempt to fully participate in the commercial world of late capitalism
while maintaining a distance that allows a critical perspective. This is a
difficult task, for artists cannot simply defy the world of commerce nor
mock it from the outside, otherwise their works may never be "consumed." Likewise, when they are completely absorbed by the commercial
world, they may lose their self-conscious awareness of their own predicament and thus become less critical. They may also begin to lose what Kuspit maintains is a touch of "primordial creativity." In his words: "Avant-
garde art lives on as the quintessential art, the most primordial art;

82
◇   neo-avant-garde art deifies it as the embodiment of purposeless primordial creativity—creativity as such, responsible only to itself" (15). Being on
the outside while remaining inside, maintaining contact with what Ulrike
Klein calls the "communication market," they try to hold on to their self-
image as "creative" artists, critics, and businesspeople (2).

Warhol and Haring fully engage the worlds of commerce and art
simultaneously. In many ways, they try not so much to mimic or mock a
particular attitude of the art world—such as the distinction between
framed art and a bicycle wheel (Duchamp) or between a painting of a
landscape and a painting of a toothbrush (Magritte)—or to focus on the
act of transaction between the artist and the collector (Yves Klein and
Boggs). Rather, they celebrate the inherent ambiguities that characterize
their own situation within contemporary culture and the community of
artists. As far as they are concerned, there seems nothing inappropriate
about a full acceptance and use of the world of manufactured commerce.
So, in the production of their work, in its content distribution, they fully
deploy that which the postindustrial world has to offer, and turn every
viewer into an art critic and every laborer into an artist. They may be
adhering to Abraham Moles's suggestion that "kitsch is essentially an aesthetic system of mass communication" wherein audience responses to
artistic objects are developed and sensitized through the exposure to
kitsch objects (Calinescu 258). (This view of kitsch defies Clement
Greenberg's dismissal that kitsch is the aesthetic opiate of the masses or
just bad art done and mass consumed in "bad taste" [1990, xx].)

This discussion of the nuances of artworks and their slippery definition or classification is lost on some critics who are still bound by the criteria of assessment used to define and classify cultural critiques and their
effective impact (or appropriateness). For example, as far as Kuspit is concerned, there is a difference between the early waves of avant-garde artists
of the twentieth century and more recent incarnations (what he refers to
as the neo-avant-garde): "But where Duchamp was enigmatic and exclusive, Warhol was obvious and inclusive: he invited his audience to be as
indifferent or uninvolved as he was" (77).

Calling Warhol an "ironic conformist" (86), Kuspit doesn't quite know
what to do with the new transformation of avant-garde expressions. It may
be easier to dismiss Kuspit's neo-avant-garde artists in comparison to the
classic or "true" avant-garde artists if one insists on a set of criteria with
which to promote and cherish their cultural contributions. As Kuspit says:
"Art today has reached a new extreme of decadence, in which it dialecti-

cally incorporates all the past signs of artistic rejuvenation—the dregs of 83
old and already won struggles for reintegration, reinvigoration—while ◇
denying their contemporary possibility" (13).

In more than one sense, avant-garde artists of the late twentieth century eschew traditional trappings of the art world while being fully cognizant of them. When Warhol chooses the photo-silk-screen process
rather than painting with oils on the traditional canvas surface, or when
Haring chooses to cover blank advertising panels in subway stations with
graffiti, they both conform to the reality of an art world different from the
one they learned from or read about. Their deliberate endorsement of new
mediums of art production plays into the hands of those who claim the
dominance of capitalism in commercial and fine art in the postmodern
age. This endorsement is interlaced with their choices of subject matter
as well. Whether it is Brillo pads or Campbell's soup cans, the familiarity
that a large portion of the public has with these icons and symbols gives
these artists a cultural access that may have been confined or limited in
previous ages.

Even Arthur Danto pays attention to Warhol's *Brillo Box* when he
concedes: "The work vindicates its claim to be art by propounding a brash
metaphor: the brillo-box-as-work-of-art." But he continues: "And in the
end this transfiguration of a commonplace object transforms nothing in
the artworld. It only brings to consciousness the structures of art which,
to be sure, requires a certain historical development before that
metaphor was possible. The moment it was possible, something like the
Brillo Box was inevitable and pointless." After this dismissal, Danto
retracts a bit and is willing to admit that "as a work of art" Warhol's *Brillo
Box* is not merely an instantiation of a particular cultural junction, where
a certain metaphor becomes not only possible but also inevitable. In fact,
it is a typical and therefore important piece of art: "It does what works of
art have always done—externalizing a way of viewing the world, expressing the interior of a cultural period, offering itself as a mirror to catch the
conscience of our kings" (1981, 208).

Once avant-garde artists blur the distinction between high and low
art through a legitimation of commercialized art and advertisement, they
turn the public's attention to preconceived notions of what constitutes a
work of art and where it ought to be displayed. What Danto and scores of
other art critics forget in their zeal to define art as separate from other
cultural expressions is the simple conditions under which objects are
accepted or rejected by the general public as good or bad expressions of

84
◇
their own tastes. For the collector to bring home the Brillo box now under the guise of art does more than legitimate the work of housekeepers; the purchase and collection explain in direct terms the aesthetic power and appeal that many objects have to those who confront them daily.

In 1955, Warhol, then a successful commercial illustrator, received his biggest advertising commission for "a weekly ad in the society pages of the Sunday *New York Times* for the fashionable Manhattan shoe store I. Miller" (Bockris 82). During 1956, while still working as a commercial (graphic) artist, Warhol pursued recognition and legitimacy as a fine artist and had his breakthrough exhibition, the "Golden Slippers," at Bodley Gallery. In this show he exhibited blotted-line drawings of shoes (the exact style of his advertising illustrations for the I. Miller campaign), except that these drawing were now leafed in gold and framed (Honnef 27ff). The shift from one medium of artistic expression, an advertisement in daily newsprint, to that of a gallery illustrates most clearly Warhol's desire for artistic validation and personal recognition. It is no longer the artist at the service of a shoe store, but a gallery at the service of an artist. The addition of gold leaf to mundane shoes transforms their aesthetic status, just as Cinderella's glass slipper became a symbol for aristocratic pretense. Warhol's use of gold is different from Klein's insofar as he retains his focus on the work of art rather than shifting it to its medium of exchange. But perhaps it is a recollection of the story of the golden calf, where earrings (like shoes) were elevated beyond their practical and aesthetic levels to a spiritual and religious level of worship and idolation.

Michele Bogart has the following insight in the context of the collapse of fine and commercial art, or in relation to the continued aspiration of retaining a fine-art status in the face of commercial success:

> [Warhol's] final product was not a reproduction, nor an advertisement, but a single canvas, a scintillating configuration of vibrating colors and shape patterns. The image confirmed the persistence and force of "fine art" ideology even as it mocked these elite and transcendental ideals.
>
> From the perspective of this study, Warhol's art represented the culmination of dilemmas about the relationship of art, media, and advertising that artists had confronted since the turn of the century. Warhol's art and career also represented a shrewd and effective public articulation of those dilemmas as they affected artists circa 1960. He forged an art and an artistic persona predi-

cated on the clash of traditional but persistent romantic ideals
with the equally persistent collapse of distinctions between "Art
Art" and "Business Art." (300)

What is striking about Warhol's chutzpa is that he collapses two worlds
that pretend to be completely separate from each other; his strategy
includes tricky instruments that bring the two worlds closer and yet highlight their differences, drawing attention to the need for artificially constructed bridges. This serious playfulness across the great cultural divide
between the worlds of commercial art and fine art has also been engaged
in by Jenny Holzer in her marquees-texts that were displayed in Times
Square and next to Caesar's Palace (her *Truism Series* of 1977–87).
Holzer's work continues Warhol's legacy of the collapsing or bridging of
the two worlds insofar as her signs have an advertising component as well
as making an artistic statement.

When Magritte produces ads for Alfa Romeo or other commercial
entities, he does not display them in a gallery—they remain what they are:
commercial products, art in the service of the world of commerce. But,
Warhol seems to argue, if the world of commerce relies on art to expand
its markets and develop new consumer needs, if artistic creations underlie the development of the marketplace, why not make them central to
that world? Why not focus on them—art objects—rather than on what
they promote—mass-produced objects? This argument is similar to the
one made by Boggs insofar as they both conflate the status of one set of
objects with the other.

As mentioned previously, when Boggs creates bank notes he draws
our attention to the artistic value that these notes have in addition to or
regardless of their face value. In a similar fashion, Warhol and Haring
illustrate and demonstrate the artistic value of commercials and advertisements by framing and marketing their art outside the "normal" commercial channels of ad campaigns and marketing firms. Once these pieces
find their way into galleries and museums, their cultural status changes
overnight. Insisting that a bottle of Coca-Cola is beautiful in and of itself,
that its contours and red label are aesthetically pleasing, Warhol reminds
his audience that a bottle of sweet bubbly syrup is also a cultural icon
(recognized domestically and internationally) whose value transcends its
use and exchange values.

Warhol's views and artistic expressions defy standard critical assessments, since they try to respond to a variety of questions simultaneously:

86 the relationship between the art world and the business world, the role of
◇ the artist, the status of originality and authenticity in the face of mechanical reproduction, and others. Klaus Honnef summarizes Warhol's precarious position during the 1950s and 1960s in this way: "The artist's strategy has certain subversive features. He undermines the hitherto
unassailable importance of uniqueness and originality as criteria for great
art—inalienable to the sense of self of contemporary art, whether avant-
garde or not. He deceives his critics with an amazing simulation, and still
contrives to retain originality as an aesthetic category" (55).

Honnef's observation about the awkward response of critics to artists
such as Warhol should remind us of the entire theoretical edifice constructed by intellectuals and critics after the fact of artistic creations. As
Renato Poggioli points out, the promotion of and sympathy for avant-
garde artwork is usually limited to a small group of intellectuals whose
privileged position and assessment oppose a "far more vast and amorphous public" that is understood to be "congenitally unfit to grasp it"
(150). When an artist such as Warhol tries to appease or appeal to these
two publics at once, both groups will reject him at first; only with the passage of time and the ability to ignore critical icons such as Greenberg will
the two publics meet at the same museum or bookstore and appreciate
the portrayal of Coca-Cola bottles and buy the poster or the T-shirt.
Warhol even comes close to Benjamin's concern with the emancipatory
potential of the arts when he suggests that Coke has a leveling power—
the power to equalize unequals—that may escape the critics' attention:
"What's great about this country is that America started the tradition
where the richest consumers buy essentially the same things as the poor-
est. You can be watching TV and see Coca-Cola, and you can know that
the President drinks Coke, Liz Taylor drinks Coke, and just think, you can
drink Coke, too. A Coke is a Coke and no amount of money can get you
a better Coke than the one the bum on the corner is drinking" (1975,
100–101).

Commercialized technoscience, then, is not the culprit that distances
us from the loftier goals of the Frankfurt school, but a wonderful and profound instrument for finding common denominators among all people.
That which is mechanically reproduced may seem to lose its political and
aesthetic force, according to some readings of Benjamin, but on our reading (following Warhol's "reproductions") it is exactly what may help bridge
class gaps and struggles so much so that underlying consumption patterns
would emerge into public and cultural consciousness.

Warhol also reminds his audience that, as Fritz Machlup explains, "The arts cannot live on what the market can offer." That is, the fine arts cannot be left to the forces of supply and demand dictated in the capitalist world. Machlup continues: "The demand is relatively small because the number of buyers is severely limited since, as a rule, the taste for the higher arts is acquired only with considerable intellectual effort and the amount each buyer can take is not elastic" (244). Machlup adds that the historical model of aristocratic and religious subsidies is no longer operational, and therefore it may be time for governments to subsidize the "higher arts." Warhol takes to heart this explanatory model, and seems to agree with Machlup's judgment that the acquisition of so-called higher tastes requires an effort most of the public is not willing to put forth. What is his solution?

Instead of begging for government subsidy (manipulating the forces of market demand for the arts), and agreeing with Machlup that the supply of art is always high (because of the psychological pleasure of artistic creation), Warhol sets out to increase the demand for the arts by an ever larger segment of the public. Rather than demanding the intellectual effort of the public to appreciate the subtleties of art history in its current incarnation, he makes the latest artistic creation as accessible as possible. What image does the public recognize? What is familiar, and therefore not threatening? Tabloid celebrities, consumer goods, and the money used to purchase them! In a consumer society one can assume the public knows its objects of pleasure and has the taste for their consumption; all that needs to be added is the appreciation of the aesthetic value of the experience of consumption. This artistic shift of emphasis is similar to Boggs's aesthetization of money and dollar bills (as mentioned in chapter 2).

Warhol's works follow Benjamin's complex response to the forces of capitalism and mechanical reproduction rather than John Berger's indictment of artistic complicity with the captains of industry, the powerful bourgeoisie. Instead of creating oil paintings to represent the material possessions of capitalists as more real and therefore more desirable than the simple possessions of the proletariat (and thereby legitimating class structure and the accumulation of wealth), Warhol uses blurred photo-silk-screen images to flatten the depths of class struggle to the media dimensionality of material consumption. While the artists of Berger's critique focus on the high-end "object of possession" (such as naked women), Warhol focuses on the middle-class encounters with daily consumption. Using the most sophisticated (art) "factory" in New York City, he legitimates the pleasures of the public—he is accessible to anyone who lives in America.

This American accessibility is in fact a consumer accessibility, and that kind of accessibility is immediately international (because American culture and its icons have been widely exported since World War II). And, unlike Berger's (status objects) oil painters, Warhol provides reproductions of his (reproductive) works so that anyone can purchase them at modest prices. In this sense, then, he plays right into the hands of capitalism and does not pretend that artists are either exempt from its market forces or can divert them to assist the cause of the proletariat. Warhol walks a tightrope between yearning for the recognition of a so-called fine artist—someone whose works are displayed in galleries, acknowledged by curators of prestigious museums, noted by art critics, and therefore collected by the rich—and undermining that recognition by making his works accessible to the masses. He provides a full circle between a so-called fine-art piece (any of his silk-screened commercial label images), a commercial or advertisement (such as his I. Miller shoe images), and an interesting hybrid of fine- and commercial-art images (such as his record labels/covers), using his distinctive realistic pop representations (O'Brien 43–51). Is this a Benjamin-like lament, or the sort of detached engagement, the duplicity of the avant-garde, as we have found it to be?

From Benjamin's Lament to Haring's

As Boggs's attorney in his counterfeiting case argued, there is a difference between manual and mechanical reproduction of works of art. This distinction became more of an issue by the beginning of the twentieth century, as is apparent in Benjamin's landmark essay on the topic. Benjamin's main examples were photography and film, two artistic mediums whose effectiveness and public appeal and acceptance were threatening to overshadow the art world's traditional mediums. Instead of following the details of his arguments in regard to film and photography and what we perceive as his lamentation over the loss of authenticity through classical mediums of artistic expression, we wish to highlight three issues as they relate to the avant-garde artists such as Warhol and Haring.

First, the religious or ritualistic dimension of a work of art, as Benjamin sees it. According to him:

> The uniqueness of a work of art is inseparable from its being imbedded in the fabric of tradition. . . . Originally the contextual integration of art in tradition found its expression in the cult. . . . It is significant that the existence of the work of art with reference to its aura is never entirely separated from its ritual function. In other words, the unique value of the "authentic" work of art has its basis in ritual, the location of its original use value. This ritualistic basis, however remote, is still recognizable as secularized ritual even in the most profane forms of the cult of beauty. (223–24)

What happens to the ritualistic basis of works of art in the age of mechanical reproduction? Benjamin says that this process "emancipates the work of art from its parasitical dependence on ritual." And finally, "Instead of being based on ritual, it begins to be based on another practice—politics" (ibid.). Benjamin's view of works of art and therefore the entire art world shifts from an analysis of the traditional and ritual basis this world maintains to the political realm into which it is moving. Photography and films, because their reproducibility is part of their conception and production, thereby become pliable means for political power plays, whether in the form of propaganda or enlightenment.

Second, Benjamin focuses on the interaction between the art world and the "masses," as he calls them, that is, the audience that now comes to consume the products of the art world. According to him: "Mechanical reproduction of art changes the reaction of the masses toward art. The reactionary attitude toward a Picasso painting changes into the progressive reaction toward a Chaplin movie. The progressive reaction is characterized by the direct, intimate fusion of visual and emotional enjoyment with the orientation of the expert. Such fusion is of great social significance" (234).

Benjamin still has in mind the problematic shift from traditional paintings to films (in terms of aura and authenticity), but his point nonetheless is worth pursuing. The notion of high art, that is, a reified painting by a famous artist, typically displayed in a fashionable and expensive gallery or museum, is being challenged by art forms whose accessibility sets the conditions for a different kind of audience participation (as in the case of Warhol). Though still spectators, audiences under the conditions of mechanical reproduction can more readily express their emotional reaction and enjoy the work of art on their terms, in their homes. Benjamin's replacement of a reactionary with a progressive attitude may be too simplistic and optimistic, but it tries to more accurately represent the shift toward the validation of so-called low art as worthy of critical engagement.

Third, the blurring of the alleged rigid distinction between high and low art is accomplished through the participation of the masses in the art world. As Benjamin puts it: "The mass is a matrix from which all traditional behavior toward works of art issues today in a new form. Quantity has been transmuted into quality. The greatly increased mass of participants has produced a change in the mode of participation" (239). Benjamin seems to allude not only to the blurring of the distinction between high and low art, but also to the reconfiguration of the entire art world in light of greater participation by the public. The fact that artworks are reproduced in the millions, the fact that art can be and is consumed not only in public places but also in the homes of millions of people—that is, the fact that art is not limited to the consumption of popes and princes— makes a big qualitative difference in the very meaning of works of art. This is not to say that collectors, critics, and curators do not wield enormous power over the distribution of works of art. Rather, this is an admission that artistic connoisseurship is open to debate. According to Benjamin: "The public is an examiner, but an absent-minded one" (241). So, however important the public has become in the consumption of artworks, it is a relatively undereducated public whose judgments fall short of the standards set by experts (as Machlup admits).

We bring up these three issues not as an endorsement of Benjamin's views, but rather as starting points from which our own views can be examined. As far as we are concerned, Benjamin ends up less the Frankfurt school, Marxist radical portrayed by generations of disciples than a romantic idealist who wishes to maintain the importance of authenticity (even if only in a vague sense of the concept of an "aura") and decries the loss of spiritual transcendence. As the three issues listed above indicate, Benjamin is far from celebrating the replacement of the ritualistic standard with a political one, for in the latter he finds as much danger as Marx found in the former. Fascism or not, the politics of art seems a standard without objectivity or transcendence. Moreover, the blurring of the distinction between high and low art lends no comfort to Benjamin, who still values the aura of authenticity. And finally, leaving art to the masses entails leaving it without the guardians of taste, lowering the threshold of aesthetic value too much for a bourgeois connoisseur such as Benjamin.

Since Benjamin's essay set the tone for the critical engagement with art in the twentieth century, we deliberate over its message and find it more complex than commonly understood. Benjamin could have made his lament more explicit and his ambivalence more sharp so that generations of artists would have more openly admitted their own predicament, their political straitjacket. What does it mean to replace the standard of ritual and tradition with politics? Isn't the political standard no different in its spiritual pretense? Isn't the political world a world of tradition, rituals, ceremonies, and power plays? And how does the economic dimension cross these boundaries? Is it indeed the case that aesthetic judgments are in fact justifications for people's tastes and preferences, and as such differ little from the kind of political judgments we make in regard to political leaders and their policies after they succeed or fail?

If the above questions are deemed rhetorical, it is because we intend to suggest in what follows that there is an economic (and thereby a political) dimension to the art world that may obscure all other, more refined aesthetic decisions made by artists, even those we consider avant-garde, and those who collect their work. Those chronicling the increase and decrease in the monetary value of works of art know that they are playing the political game of celebrity status. Name recognition, marketing blitzes, and one-person shows in galleries and museums are political through and through, since setting a rigid standard of qualitative difference is impossible in principle and in practice. So, whoever can invest more money in promotion and advertising is bound to get better results, just as in political campaigns. If advertisement is the name of the game (of success and happiness), then why not turn the tables and make advertisements themselves into objects worthy of aesthetic consideration, as Warhol does in his "Golden Slippers" show.

Incidentally, Toulouse-Lautrec, whose exhibition of his cabaret posters in the official salons was an exception to his contemporaries and to his own body of work, was more of an anomaly than the standard of the late nineteenth century. Warhol, by contrast, makes this issue—the display of one sort of art in another space—his main object. He thereby also continues Duchamp's defiance of the rules of gallery exhibition (what is allowed to be hung side by side for public viewing). Haring continues this defiance as well, but goes outside the walls of the gallery and displays his works on commercial panels in subway stations. As we shall see in the next chapter, blurring the boundaries of exhibition spaces becomes itself the focus of the works of some artists (performance artists and others) such as the Christos.

Despite Benjamin's lament, and probably more closely aligned with Marx's own ideals concerning the culture of the proletariat and the accessibility of art for the workers (as opposed to the cult of high art that reproduces the values of the bourgeoisie), both Warhol and Haring in their different ways celebrated the iconlike status they and their works acquired in the public's mind. Instead of remaining aloof and in the background, hidden from the public's eye by agents, brokers, curators, managers, and collectors, they made direct connections with their audiences through the media and in person. Since the labor force—the people, the masses, the public—was enjoying their works, having a so-called legitimate aesthetic experience, replacing it somewhat with its regular religious experiences, these avant-gardists showed that art need not be limited to popes and princes, the wealthy minority of every culture. Aesthetic enjoyment opened up to a variety of subgroups within the population; it became more prevalent and, dare we say, more understood, so that the accountability of artists increased. It is not that artists had to succumb to the lowest of the lowest aesthetic tastes, but rather that they had to be understood by anyone who happened to come across their work. Even when the artistic message could be read on more than one level, it had to have at least one level accessible to most people most of the time, and thereby even out the aesthetic playing ground, much like what the church has done over the past two thousand years. Theological debates may continue forever, and some ideological and aesthetic subtleties may escape most parishioners, yet one would hope that a level of understanding and appreciation will be available to anyone wishing to participate in or enjoy an experience, may it be mundane or religious.

We should note that the choice of Haring's work as opposed to the works of Neiman and Doolittle, for example, is related less to the technique they all use (in terms of cartoonlike images befitting advertisements and posters) and more to the political statements either directly made by Haring's work or indirectly inferred by his viewers. Not unlike other avant-garde artists we have mentioned, Haring appreciates the political dimension of his activity as an artist, an appreciation that is different from the standard appreciation of politics in terms of political institutions. For Haring and his viewers, there is ample room for political activism that is more contextualized in commercialized technoscience in our sense of the term. Moreover, this approach goes a long way toward our definition of avant-garde artworks in terms of subversion and appropriation rather than in terms of confrontational defiance. Finally, this approach is more easily explained in light of the commercial and cultural success Haring (and Warhol before him) could enjoy, while all along maintaining his detached engagement.

The populist approach of Warhol and Haring begins with: Have you ever gone to the grocery store? Have you ever seen a can of soup? Have you ever ridden a subway or a train? Have you ever seen graffiti? The underlying questions start the artistic conversation Warhol and Haring have with their viewers. Once the questions are answered in the affirmative, the rest of the conversation seems less alienating or intimidating. In fact, the close attention to the public and its commercial taste becomes the underlying framework for artists such as Haring. John Gruen quotes Haring as saying: "Because I was riding the subways every day to go to work and also to look at graffiti, I started to notice all the ads in the stations. . . . It was also at that time that I saw my first empty black panels. These black paper panels were used to cover up old advertisements. . . . As I kept seeing these black subway panels everywhere, I realized what I had discovered. Suddenly, everything fell into place" (68).

Haring views the blank advertising panels in the public space of the subway stations as "his" space, the way Renaissance artists viewed church walls as "their" spaces to be marked, painted, and foregrounded. The entertainer Madonna continues this line of thought when she says about Haring's work: "There is this small, elite group of artists who think we are selling out. Meanwhile, the rest of the world is digging us! Of course, it is what they want too! . . . Keith didn't want to do his work for these people of New York City—he wanted to do it for everybody, everywhere. I mean, an artist wants world recognition! He wants to make an impression on the world. He doesn't just want a small, sophisticated, elitist group of people appreciating his work" (ibid. 93).

Madonna, herself an icon of the world of entertainment, finds solace in her friend's quest for fame and recognition beyond the limits of the so-called art world and its gatekeepers. For her, there is nothing tainted in Haring's exposure to a much wider audience than is common for visual artists. She confesses what Stephan and Levin understand as the motivation for the work of scientists, namely, world recognition and the wealth that accompanies that recognition. She also defies the elite consumers whose judgments alone no longer determine aesthetic value. She

94 applauds her friend Haring not for being yet another graffiti artist, but for
◇ elevating his graffiti art into a legitimate form of artistic expression, one
that is universally accessible and aesthetically pleasing. He, like her,
wants the public to "dig" them. Are they selling out? Or are they indeed
more responsive and thereby more respectful of the public that reveres
traditional artworks? Isn't their work more therapeutic on a social and
cultural level than any of the oil paintings hung on museum and gallery
walls? Isn't their work more effective than the insular critical discourse of
academics because it provokes the public to consider aesthetic dilemmas
and the role of art in contemporary culture?

Apprehensions about the validity of a public display of art linked to
product promotion dates to the 1920s, when critics such as Walter Pach
denounced this kind of art as "subway art." Bogart quotes Pach: "'Subway
Art does more than sell face powder and cigarettes to the crowd,' Pach
warned. 'It "sells" the art-conception of its makers to the vast majority of
people, and every rank of society.' . . . 'Subway Art' pictures narrated brief
and superficial incident, avoiding any hint of real conflict, either visual or
emotional. Its images encouraged stupor and discouraged any effort to
provide insight into life's complexities" (227–28).

It remains an open question whether or not Haring's work has been
able to respond to Pach's critique, just because the reference is not to a
particular product but rather to an artistic genre or the political concern
of a community of artists. Yet, the abstract political slogan is available as
a product, having been transformed from the subway wall drawing into a
postcard or T-shirt, and thereby is as much for sale as any product adver-
tised on subway walls. The difference, of course, is the self-referential
nature of Haring's work.

What Is Art Good For?

Calvin Tomkins, one of the leading American art critics, claims that
"of all the young artists who made it big in the eighties, Keith Haring
reached the widest audience." Part of his success is attributed to the fact
that "Haring beat the system by operating both inside and outside the art
market" (66). Known for his cartoon-style, graffiti-influenced drawings
created on blank subway advertising panels, Haring could be recognized
by thousands of viewers who would never think of entering the doors of
galleries and museums. At the same time, he was also showing in leading
galleries in New York and at international art fairs (such as Documenta

82). Perhaps another way of understanding what it means to be both inside and outside the art market is to follow the path undertaken by the artist himself, as Brooks Adams has done in reviewing Haring's journals, published posthumously in 1996. According to Adams, "His art, as we learn from the *Journals*, was not just formed by street culture but also by a voracious need to take in everything in the downtown and uptown art worlds" (35).

Just as Warhol wanted to succeed Jackson Pollock as "the American art king," according to Jerome Groopman (41), so did Haring have ideals he was to emulate in order to succeed. How ambitious these artists were in terms of their position in the history of art remains unclear, and also less interesting in this context, compared to the fact that however rebellious they were, they retained a keen eye on the art world and its changing market value. Outsiders as they were, they still kept in mind collectors and curators, enjoying the fame and monetary rewards that come with celebrity status. Concerned with communicating to a larger audience, what Machlup would call the expansion of the demand for art (and thereby an increase in its monetary value), Haring has this to say about his target audience: "The subway drawings opened my eyes to this whole other understanding of art as something that really could have an effect on and communicate to larger numbers of people that were increasingly becoming the harbors of the art. Art was a symbol of the bourgeois and the people who could afford it and 'understand' it. And it was used as a way of separating the general population from the upper class and used in a lot of ways as a tool against the rest of the population. . . . I think those barriers started being broken down by Madison Avenue, advertising, television, and Andy Warhol" (Rubell 55).

Haring acknowledges his links to Warhol in his fight for a wider audience and the legitimation of art forms that were not perceived as high art, and in his concern with the restriction of the art market (of the fine arts). But unlike Warhol, he maintains that he is "not really taken seriously because of the other things that [I do] like the Pop Shop and graphics." There may be a note of self-pity in this quote, but Haring quickly changes his tone and says: "the subway drawings were sort of my grand gesture, to say fuck you to the art market, and to say you can make these things while obviously not making money" (ibid. 55, 58).

Haring's Pop Shops were immensely popular and made him a wealthy man. From our perspective, they were an interesting but not an original extension of the museum shops that cater to the consumers of so-called

96

◇ high art. They all want a piece of the action; they all want to possess that which is valued by their culture; they want the Mona Lisa on their living room walls. And if the museum shop's reproduction is less than satisfying, then Warhol would produce a more fantastic, bigger, more colorful, and funnier facsimile. Haring says, don't worry about the Mona Lisa, just recall your favorite comic strips and the pleasures they brought to you as a child. As an adult, you can still find the child in yourself and enjoy the stories I tell through my images. You can easily and cheaply purchase them in one of my shops, and have a daily reminder of your relation to the art world.

Warhol and Haring, in their respective ways, help bring about this transition and expansion of the artistic marketplace. The consumers of aesthetic value have been increased from a small group of collectors (described in chapter 2) to a much larger group, namely, the public at large. The fact that the private lives of these artists were displayed publicly (and therefore they became celebrities and icons of pop culture) and the fact that the gay movement that began in the late 1960s deployed their images and celebrity status in order to bring its concerns before the public are immensely important but not our focus here. For what we wish to remind ourselves is not how high and low art are blurred in their works, nor how art can be used for social and political purposes. Following these paths would lead us to yet another variant of Kuspit's positive assessment of the therapeutic powers of art and the significance of avant-garde artists as promoters of social and political causes.

Here is Kuspit's thesis: "The artist is a natural therapist, as it were, and the work of art a natural medium of healing." In this sense, then, he suggests that art's "therapeutic intention becomes its context of significance, the source of its value." This means that "The conception of the avant-garde artist has become the raison d'être—at once the centerpiece, backbone, and justification—of modern art. It has been generalized into an adulatory fetishization of the artist as such. Modern thinkers have attributed special authenticity, integrity, and power to the artist" (11, 28, 2).

What bothers Kuspit, and many other, more traditional art critics who are aligned with the Clement Greenberg school of criticism, is that the salient and redeeming features associated with art as a means for cultural elevation and spiritual transcendence may not be as prominently displayed as they wish. When that happens, they sound like Kuspit: "Today, the artist remains an unconventional hero, but he is also perceived as a pretender—all too stylized and privileged in his unconventionality—if not quite a conventional fraud" (3).

The fraudulent aspects of contemporary art depend on a false reliance on postmodernism, and postmodernism turns out to be the culprit for the predicaments of modernity. Benjamin's lament and the complex responses he proposed early in the century are ignored by those critics who want a solution, an answer, a way out of the predicament. And the medicine of art seems ineffective, as far as they are concerned. Kuspit represents this way of thinking: "Postmodernism, coldblooded and calculating about art—Warhol epitomizes this 'realistic,' objective attitude—pessimistically reduces art to its own history, implicitly acknowledging art's lack of significant effect on human existence and world history" (55).

If this is the general attitude of these critics, then Warhol, like any other contemporary avant-garde artist, is condemned to receive the following indictment: "Warhol's art signals the end of the belief in the therapeutic power of art. It exists to disillusion us about art, and is an art of disillusionment. As such, it is the first genuinely postmodernist art." Postmodern art, incapable of healing, is contrasted with previous avant-garde art in which the therapeutic intent of the artist is supposed to be coupled with that of the perceiver: "Today, to be avant-garde has reversed meaning: it is to accept cynically, guiltlessly, a facile, impersonal formula for making art and being an artist, rather than to be a missionary converting the fallen to the faith of the true self by way of an original art" (ibid. 66, 74).

Using the language of religion, bemoaning the loss of the redemptive promise art could supply, Kuspit is not alone in harshly assessing the current state of affairs. But, is his lament limited to the art world and its failure to reach levels higher than those reached by the culture surrounding it? It seems that the lament is broader: "And only in a self-satisfied America could avant-garde art reify itself and become socially conformist, attaching itself to the apron strings of media sensibility, with its determination to present everything with mystifying banality" (87).

Moreover, "pseudo-avant-garde has displaced true avant-garde art as the standard-bearer of artistic significance." Kuspit's concern is with the true avant-garde artist as a "spiritual savior" and not a "worldly king." What makes the avant-garde artist pseudo is the appropriation of already accepted images and thus the reduction in the "offensive" element that is part and parcel of the true avant-garde artist. The true avant-garde artist reminds modernity of its humanity and the values that keep it as such; it

98 has to provoke and offend, recall unpleasant deviation from the spiritual
◇ path of the past, according to Kuspit. By contrast, the celebration of the
postmodern artist, the pseudo-avant-garde artist, is of the existing values
of the culture, and thus there is no challenge, however much it may seem
so on the surface (101–8).

Rosalind Krauss echoes this sentiment in her assessment of the
"appropriation" works of Sherrie Levine:

> Now, insofar as Levine's work explicitly deconstructs the mod-
> ernist notion of origin, her effort cannot be seen as an *extension*
> of modernism. It is, like the discourse of the copy, postmodernist.
> Which means that it cannot be seen as avant-garde either.
>
> Because of the critical attack it launches on the tradition
> that precedes it, we might want to see the move made in Levine's
> work as yet another step in the forward march of the avant-garde.
> But this would be mistaken. (170)

Many of the theorists and art critics of the present day indict contemporary artists for failing to fulfill a promise they never made; if anything, it is a hope of those theorists and critics that is not fulfilled. They
therefore can speak of the death of the avant-garde or the end of the
emancipatory power of art in general. But this way of thinking misses the
point. Art is now so overwhelmingly public, so open for anyone to make
claims about it and use it for whatever he or she wishes, that any standard
or limited classification of art and avant-garde art is too narrow and
thereby obsolete. (See more on this topic in chapter 5.)

The invitation to participate in the world of commercialized technoscience is one no avant-gardist can refuse to accept, as we have illustrated
in this chapter. But participation in this world may take on different
guises. It is not limited to the examples of Warhol and Haring, both of
whom commercialized their own works so as to point out the aesthetic
value of daily activities and products, and in order to broaden the scope
of artistic appreciation to a public more receptive to their displays than to
those confined to galleries and museums. Instead, it is open to other
experiments and other displays, some of which are more grandiose in size
and scope than what was available to Warhol's factory in New York City:
the public works of the Christos. Perhaps what binds them together, however different their intentions and the modes of their expressions turn out
to be, is a loose relation they seem to have. One could term this relation

the desire (noted by Kuspit to have been similar in Duchamp and Picasso)
"to be the Jew of painting, sufficiently alien to society to confront it with ◇
an alternative integrity" (Kuspit 38).

Using the language of integrity, Kuspit brings up the point made in a different context by Lyotard, namely, that when we experiment with the past in order to change the future, we must be responsible for our words and actions. This may turn out to be the only offer avant-garde art can make to the public: personal integrity in the face of collective indifference; self-conscious responsibility that defies the self-imposed limits on culpability of commercialized technoscience.

4

Unveiling the Christos

Many nights, standing in front of the western vistas, we envisioned ourselves on the threshold of a new aesthetic experience, in the presence of a new revelation.

—Cicotello and Sassower on the Christos,
with apologies to Joseph Stella

Introduction

IN ACCORDANCE with our earlier analyses, the environmental artworks of the Christos extend the detached engagement of the avant-garde with the predicaments of modernity (commercial technoscience). We should emphasize that our focus on Christo and Jeanne-Claude's temporary fabric constructions for outdoor sites is not meant as a survey or a biography. Instead, we attempt to contextualize their projects (particularly their large-scale works in the vast landscapes of the western United States) within a broader tradition than they allow in their public pronouncements, and illustrate the ways in which they have been able to escape the standard criticism launched against avant-garde art and artists (for example, that their content is too self-reflective and therefore emotionally barren, or that it is too esoteric and theoretical to have any public appeal). Rather than insisting on esoteric mediums of expression and a deliberate anti-bourgeois posture, the Christos make their outdoor art a public spectacle accessible to the widest possible audience. Viewing this spectacle, moreover, does not require a "ticket," as Christo proudly states. And finally, the free public accessibility of their large-scale projects adds an enigmatic dimension to the often perplexing experience of the hermetically bound and critically profound avant-garde art. As a fellow artist, Robert Arenson, says: "When the fence [Christo's *Running Fence, Sonoma and Marin Counties, California 1972–76*] was up it was great! The check-out ladies in the supermarket were arguing about the definition of art" (Fineberg 357, 359). Arenson's comments reflect a positive assessment of the Christos' ability to break down the elitist confines of contemporary art. The Christos reverse the typical marketing strategy of the exclusive, even elusive specter of avant-garde art and experience, as seen with Klein and Boggs, by inviting everyone to participate and partake in their artistic offering.

Is this what makes the Christos phenomenon an avant-garde enigma? The enigmatic character of the large-scale Christos projects can be summarized with the following set of questions. If they were to be cast as modernists, the retort would be that the Christos aren't elitist; if they were to be cast as postmodernists, then the retort would be that the projects have spiritual aspirations; if they were to be accused of being theorists, the response would be that their works are handmade, humanmade, and actually constructed; if they were to be labeled spiritualists, they could respond that the projects engage the material landscape and the real world; if they were to be labeled capitalists, they'd claim to be poor populists; if they were accused of commercialism, the reply would be that they are filling a shared idealist void; and finally, if they were labeled self-promoters, they could easily point to their privately financed and constructed projects and the projects' extensive impact on others.

From another perspective, the Christos embody a phenomenon that is paradoxical (as well as enigmatic). On the one hand, the public has great expectations for and celebrates the accomplishments of avant-garde artists as critics and revolutionaries, creative geniuses and visionary idealists. On the other hand, the public fears the wrath of artists (in the sense of being mocked as philistines) and wishes them to bow to and abide by the conventions of socialized commercialism. The predicament facing every artist is clear: go outside the institutionalized establishment in order to impress the public and make your mark, but have no illusion that your work will be accepted and funded. And if only the starry-eyed and idealistic young or the already established and well-to-do old can be counted on to accept the predicament as a challenge worth pursuing, then we are in trouble. The young may know too little to appreciate what it means to cross boundaries and stretch the limits of tradition, and the old may be too cynical to care about doing so.

Perhaps what makes the enigma called the Christos so fascinating is their defiance of Walter Benjamin's lament. But, unlike Warhol's popular appeal that retains its dependence on particular art objects, the Christos

102
◇

provide their audiences a once-in-a-lifetime experience, or what one may call a shared but individualized public experience of the sublime. There is no mechanical reproduction in their works: they are unique and ephemeral. There is no confusion between the original and its copies. Anyone can volunteer to help make the one original, and thereby participate in an act of unequaled authenticity—it's almost like being in Michelangelo's workshop, or working on the Sistine Chapel! Here they are, the unassuming Christos, challenging in their actions and not in their words the warning and lament of Benjamin and his leftist disciples. What is being challenged is the notion of lost authenticity in the age of mechanical reproduction.

At the same time, one is left with the following question: what is one to make of artists who want to challenge the enduring monuments of the past—the pyramids, the Great Wall, classical temples—as the Christos do with architectural, even environmental art that is deliberately transitory? We consider the answer to be the temporal and fairly immediate erasure of their monumental projects. Perhaps the temporality of existence of these artworks may explain a way out of the paradoxical role undertaken by the Christos. As Marina Vaizey has pointed out, the Christos continue to help us appreciate the temporality of the artistic experience (Baal-Teshuva 52). This appreciation is traceable to Kant's notion of the sublime and its contemporary reiteration by Jean-François Lyotard. As David Nye points out in regard to different conceptions of the sublime: "From Burke to Kant to later thinkers, the natural world plays a smaller and smaller role in the definitions of the sublime, and the observer becomes central in defining the emotion as the mind projects its interior state on the world. Burke insisted on the centrality of the natural scene in invoking the sublime. Kant emphasized that the mind was central in apprehending the sublime, thus shifting attention from physical nature to its perception" (8).

The current revival of Kant's notion of the sublime by numerous art critics, art historians, aestheticians, and cultural critics (such as de Duve) testifies to the ongoing quest for spiritual deliverance. Kant supports a postmodern shift in emphasis when judging works of art on a variety of levels. First, there is a recognition that the definition and matrices of artworks have expanded and engulf a variety of objects and subjects. Second, it is understood that a multitude of interpretations are bound to surround anything artistic. And third, the analytic evaluation of artworks is overshadowed by an artistic experience that remains personal and at times inexplicable. Though critical judgment is partially bound by an intellectual reflection, its ultimate foundation eludes linguistic explanation. Thus Kant's insistence on the sublime is an irresistible base for the establishment of a permanent and ultimate foundation for all interpretations.

The foundation sought by intellectuals, academics, clerics, and lay people can be understood in a variety of ways given different languages and contexts. That is to say, whether one is a priest or an artist, there remains a desire to provide one's audience with simple, concrete answers to the ambiguities of modernity. Postmodernity, with all its fanfare, cannot be the resting ground sought by leaders of the modern day, because it opens up questions, it provides too many paths and answers all of which are claimed to be equally legitimate. So, by the beginning of the twenty-first century, with a culture of rampant pluralism, one is more confused than ever, more at a loss not only about what to think, but also what to do. If one adds to this general existential condition of anxiety the economic hardships of postindustrial unemployment and the technological proliferation that increase the gap between the rich (nations) and the poor (nations), it is no surprise that the quest for a definitive answer, a foundation, or a transcendence would ring ever so loud.

From this perspective of yearning toward a resolution of questions about the paradoxes of modernity, the renewed interest in the inexplicability of the aesthetic experience, its sense of awe, is bound to resurface. One can therefore understand wide public support for the projects of the Christos: pointing toward god, God, or the sublime. (As we shall see, the Christos play off the notion of a Christ-like art and artist who can deliver humanity from its current traumas.) The temporality of their projects—as opposed to enduring natural phenomena such as Niagara Falls—adds a dimension of urgency to the experience of the sublime. For instance, Albert Elsen says the following: "Christo believes the temporary nature of his projects gives them more energy and intensifies our response. . . . Again and again, temporariness becomes the issue" (Baal-Teshuva 47). In an appearance at the Fine Arts Center in Colorado Springs (29 June 1998), the Christos said as much: "The temporality of our art creates an urgency to be seen, the work has a presence of being missed, not there in the future." The temporal "interruptions" or "gentle disturbances" that are launched on nature by the Christos have a certain marketing angle: come to see the work right now, because if you wait too long it won't be there anymore!

The appeal of the temporality of the aesthetic experience for the public

104
◇ and its accompanying conception of aesthetic awe are similar to what some regard as spiritual or religious experience, whether in William James's sense of a personal experience or a tele-evangelist's sense of public proportion. As Nye explains about the particular characteristics of American culture's reception of the sublime experience in nature:

> The development of Niagara Falls and the Natural Bridge as tourist sites [in the late nineteenth century] suggests some of the ways in which Americans adapted the sublime to their own society. Although in philosophical discussions the sublime is usually treated as an emotion enjoyed in solitude, in America it has quite often been experienced in a crowd. Natural wonders are usually surrounded by tourists, and virtually every technological demonstration, such as a world's fair or a rocket launch, provides a sublime experience for a multitude. . . . The presence of a crowd can enhance the interest in an object, confirming its importance. The psychology of the crowd creates additional meanings. (27)

Nye dismisses the standard complaints about how crowds and commercial promotions vulgarize the solitude many claim necessary for sublime experiences. Instead of finding public facilities obtrusive on the solitary experience of the sublime, he explains the necessary conditions that these facilities provide in order for nature and/or technological objects to be experienced as sublime.

Comparing tourist adventures into nature to a Cape Canaveral launch to religious experiences, Nye says: "Though the sublime object might be a part of a tour package, the experience itself cannot be guaranteed to occur. One had to do more than just pay the price of admission; like a religious penitent intent on grace, one had to be receptive and patient as well" (28). How do Nye's analysis and critique mesh with the public's perception of the Christos' many large-scale projects, such as *Running Fence*? Though Christo claims that "with our art you do not need tickets to see it" (Baal-Teshuva 92), he and his wife are ardent self-promoters and persistent salespeople of their projects (some take as many as twenty years to bring to fruition, because of the legal and logistical problems that require licenses and permits from a variety of government agencies).

Moreover, the Christos are acutely aware of the ideological masks

worn by cultural leaders and insist on unveiling them. One area where
this unveiling is most pronounced is their environmental works in the
American West. Perhaps what makes these works more interesting as spiritual aids is their location in "pristine" environments where only "natural"
objects are expected. Though wrapping the Reichstag in Berlin (1995) may
have strong impact as an ideological critique, it is an activity that could
simply be undertaken for safety during renovation or construction. The
Christos' shift from Europe to the United States, from the urban setting
of wrapped buildings, small-scale packages, oil-barrel sculptures, and covered ancient walls to landscape projects in the western U.S., embodies
and captures broader shifts in our perception of the development of Western art. The transformation of their projects after moving to America (the
"shift to an architectural scale" in Fineberg's sense, 353) parallels the transition from Mediterranean classical tradition of figurative objects to the
new experimental media canons of the international avant-garde.

Are the Christos captive to the individualistic, adventurous, and
hopeful "myth of the American West"? Do they attempt to fulfill the
promise of the sublime or the material promise of manifest destiny? Western religious art depicts the solitude of baptism as a personal salvation;
Christo (the "idea man" of this pair, as Jeanne-Claude is quick to
acknowledge) baptizes the western American land on a grand scale. Into
which community of belief are the Christos initiating us? Theirs is a
vision no cleric ever envisioned. Is their newly found beauty of the West
an authentication of the quest for the sublime already framed by nineteenth-century landscape painters? Is it a continuation of this quest for
transcendence? As we attempt to answer these questions, we will analyze
the ideological underpinnings that have made the West so attractive to
American landscape painters of the nineteenth century as well as to the
Christos.

Western tradition has viewed miracle-makers as those who cater to
individuals (Jesus the healer) or to groups (Moses at Mount Sinai). In secular settings there have been revolutionary figures who helped transform
their societies and in that sense performed miracles (Gandhi and Martin
Luther King, for example). In their work, artists compete with divine creations and the products of political leaders and captains of industry. Yet,
they have a unique place in our culture as those who provide refuge from
daily suffering and misery with objects of sublime beauty. Is it a moment
of escape? Is the temporality of the aesthetic experience good enough to

provide a safe haven for the needy? What power can art have in the present day? Can it rival religion and science, or does it use religion and science to empower itself?

Nye responds in the affirmative to these questions because of the
ongoing transformation of the notion and experience of the sublime. Nye
would agree that sublime-oriented projects like those of the Christos
indeed take their audiences outside the confines of the cathedrals and
museums and bring them closer to nature and to God. (One can see this
transformation also in the avant-garde architecture of Frank Lloyd
Wright, including Fallingwater [1935] and his Unitarian church [1947];
see Costantino.) But, regardless of the ongoing transformation of the
examples and experience of the sublime, one can detect certain features
or a structure that permeates all the phenomena commonly labeled the
sublime. As Nye says, "[The sublime experience to modern people], when
it occurs, has a basic structure. An object, natural or man-made, disrupts
ordinary perception and astonishes the senses, forcing the observer to
grapple mentally with its immensity and power. This amazement occurs
most easily when the observer is not prepared for it; however, like religious conversion at a camp meeting it can also occur over a period of days
as internal resistance melts away" (15–16). Understood aesthetically or
religiously, the sublime leaves one awed and inspired, confused and hopeful. What fascinates us in this context is the technoscientific scaffolding
that retains its vitality and influence, its immense power and appeal.

The Technoscientific Sublime

Edmund Burke, the eighteenth-century theoretician of the sublime,
did not limit the transcendental experience of the sublime to sensations
evoked solely by viewing natural phenomena. He noted that the experience can be evoked through human-made objects, such as monumental
architectural structures. Nye quotes Burke as saying, "When any work
seems to have required immense force and labour to effect it, the idea is
grand." Nye comments: "Burke also notes that size alone does not explain
completely the effect of the architecture on the imagination" (85–86).

One can move from one sort of technoscientific sublime to another,
from awe-inspired appreciation of the sheer size of structures (already
apparent in the eighteenth century) to the internal workings of structures
and the machinery that activates them (after the industrial revolution). As

Nye tells it, the writer John Pendleton Kennedy remarked on the sublime 107
aspects of the "early modern factory" that presented the viewer with vast ◇
stretches of machinery and assembly lines that seemed to extend to infin-
ity. "Kennedy comments that he was 'lost in admiration' before 'the vast
engineering' and 'the infinite complication of wheels' in the factory" (114).

There is yet another shift in the appreciation of the sublime, one that
moves from the machinery itself to acknowledging the sublimity of those
who operate it, those who are, in Marx's and Charlie Chaplin's sense,
nothing but an extension of the machine. As Nye notes: "Yet for many the
most impressive fact of the mills was not the [sublime] architecture, the
[sublime] intricate machinery, or the [sublime] vast production, but the
cohorts of workers who seemed to be marshaled into an ideal order. . . .
The casual visitor may have seen the mill as sublime demonstration of
man's ingeniousness and superior intellect" (115). Nye's observations are
relevant to the assessment of the Christos as creators of sublime experience because they add to it the quantitative measurements used to support qualitative judgments. That is to say, to appreciate the sublime
aspects of mechanical production, one needs to appreciate the immense
quantities of materials, energy, and labor that go into the production of
huge quantities of consumable items. This appreciation can be accomplished, in Christo's sense, with their complex visual proposals accompanied by their long and detailed news releases.

Note the following facts concerning some of the Christos' projects;
they are valuable tools with which to measure the phenomenon of the
sublime as experienced by those working on these projects, as well as the
eventual audience. The Christos' *Running Fence* of 1972–76 stretched 24.5
miles and was 18 feet high. It was smaller than any transcontinental rail-
way built to cross the West; it was shorter than any poles of electrical lines
found across the western landscape. We quote here from the Christos'
press releases, since their self-promotion provides extensive information
about their works. Here is a more detailed description of the 1991
Umbrella Project:

> At sunrise, on October 9th, 1991, Christo's 1,880 workers began to
> open the 3,100 Umbrellas in Ibaraki and California, in the pres-
> ence of the artist.
> This Japan-USA temporary work of art reflects the similari-
> ties and differences in the ways of life and the use of the land in

two inland valleys, one 19 kilometers long (12 miles) in Japan, and the other 29 kilometers long (18 miles) in the USA. . . .

Eleven manufacturers in Japan, USA, Germany and Canada prepared the various elements of the Umbrellas: Fabric, aluminum super-structure, steel frame bases, anchors, wooden base supports, bags and molded base covers.

Starting in December 1990, with a total work force of 500, Muto Construction Co. Ltd. in Ibaraki, and A. L. Huber & Son in California installed the earth anchors and steel bases. The sitting platform/base covers were placed during August and September 1991.

From September 19 to October 7, 1991, an additional construction work force began transporting the Umbrellas to their assigned bases, bolted them to the receiving sleeves, and elevated the Umbrellas to an upright closed position. On October 4, students, agricultural workers, and friends, 960 in USA and 920 in Japan, joined the work force to complete the installation of the Umbrellas.

Christo's 26 million dollar temporary work of art is entirely financed by the artist through The Umbrellas, Joint Project for Japan and U.S.A. Corporation (Jeanne-Claude Christo-Javacheff, president). Previous projects by the artist have all been financed in a similar manner through the sale of his studies, preparatory drawings, collages, scale models, early works, and original lithographs. The artist does not accept any sponsorship.

The removal will start on October 31 and the land will be restored to its original condition. The Umbrellas will be taken apart and all elements will be recycled.

The Umbrellas, freestanding dynamic modules, reflect the availability of the land in each valley, creating an invitational inner space, as houses without walls, or temporary settlements and relate to the ephemeral character of the work of art. In the precious and limited space of Japan, the Umbrellas are positioned intimately, close together and sometimes following the geometry of the rice fields. In the luxuriant vegetation enriched by water year round, the Umbrellas are blue. In the California vastness of uncultivated grazing land, the configuration of the

Umbrellas is whimsical and spreading in every direction. The
brown hills are covered by blond grass, and in that dry landscape,
the Umbrellas are yellow.

From October 9th, 1991 for a period of three weeks, *The
Umbrellas* will be seen, approached, and enjoyed by the public,
either by car from a distance and closer as they border the roads,
or by walking under *The Umbrellas* in their luminous shadows.

Let us review some of the elements of this project. *The performance:* $26
million for a display that lasts only three weeks; 1,880 installation workers;
construction work force of 500; 3,100 umbrellas; 2,000 gallons of paint;
4,413,347 square feet of fabric; total of 1,655,400 pieces. *The message:* invitational inner space, the ephemeral character of the work of art. *The commercial:* personally financed, no sponsorship accepted. (For a detailed discussion of the economics of environmental artists such as the Christos,
their insistence on representing themselves and not using managers, and
their creation of entrepreneurial organizations for the production and dissemination of their work, see Deitch 85–91.) *The aftermath:* land restored
to its original condition, all elements recycled. *The capitalist take:* capitalist conquest of nature is tenable. *The marketing:* whatever you do, present yourself as doing it with private funds, but make sure thousands want
to jump on your bandwagon. *The moral of the story:* you think it's cultural
critique and art, but it's really about old-time religion for the future with
the Christos as prophets and high priests. Our assessment is neither out-
landish nor sarcastic; read again the first paragraph of the press release
quoted above: "At sunrise, on October 9th, 1991, Christo's 1,880 workers
began to open the 3,100 Umbrellas in Ibaraki and California, in the presence of the artist." Only God or Christ could have been present simultaneously at Ibaraki and California. Perhaps right then and there (where
exactly?) we had our Second Coming. Perhaps Christo is Christ; the news
release says so! Or, perhaps the explanation is as mundane as the difference in time zones and the speed of airplanes.

In addition, what we call the technoscientific sublime is easily accessible to the public through the promotional and marketing strategies used
by the Christos. They impress the public through the media with the kind
of statistical data churned out by corporate America or national data
bureaus so that their prestige and power is validated and indirectly
endorsed. But unlike some promoters and marketing executives, the

110
◇

Christos indeed fabricate and build the monuments that they promise, providing the public the experience of Nye's industrial sublime:

> The industrial sublime combined the abstraction of a man-made landscape with the dynamism of moving machinery and powerful forces. The factory district, typically viewed from a high place or from a moving train, thus combined the dynamic and the geometrical sublimes. The synthesis evoked fear tinged with wonder. It threatened the individual with its sheer scale, its noise, its complexity, and the superhuman power of the forces at work. Yet, as with other forms of the technological sublime, this scene ultimately reaffirmed the power of reason—but not in Kant's sense. Rather than provoke an inward meditation that arrived at a transcendental deduction applicable to humanity as a whole, these landscapes forced onlookers to respect the power of the corporation and the intelligence of its engineers [and artists]. (Nye 126)

Nye seems to agree with our analysis of the lament over modernity and the inability of postmodernity to provide the conditions for simple answers and sublime experiences. He shows clearly why Kant's ideals and hope, reflected as they were in the rest of the Enlightenment leadership, could not be materialized where one expected them to be realized, especially with the advent of the industrial revolution. Technoscience should have provided the conditions of surplus, in Marx's sense, so that the individual could have the leisure time to reflect and enjoy the beauty of nature and culture. This could lead to introspective enlightenment, enjoyment of reason and aesthetics alike, rather than the resulting brooding anxiety found in some critical assessments of modernity. Instead, what one has by the end of the twentieth century is a set of industrial products some of which are more frightening than ever: the atomic bomb, Zyklon-B (used in concentration camps during World War II), and the cloning potential of biomedicine.

Though different in character from Benjamin's lament over the role of mechanical reproduction in twentieth-century culture, Nye's lament is just as powerful and painful: he wishes for technoscience to help bring about that which it cannot. Nye says: "In Kantian terms the sublime event is, of course, that which is absolutely great. But [witnesses to NASA launches] differ from Kant in their interpretation of the sublime object. Whereas Kant postulated the realization of reason through the experience of the absolutely great in nature, the pilgrim to Cape Canaveral realizes patriotism through the experience of the absolutely great in technology" (241).

What is Nye left with? For him, all we can hope for, even when we observe the most wonderful natural phenomena, is the "consumer's sublime." In his words:

> The paradox of the technological sublime is that it pretends to present legible materialization of the unrepresentable—as though a physical construction could be infinite, as though the boundless could be bounded, as though the shapeless could be shaped. . . . For Kant the hurricane was not a concretization of reason, but Americans have long thought that new machines are nothing less than that. For Kant the natural sublime object evokes the feeling of enthusiasm, or a pleasure of a purely negative kind, for it finally concerns a failure of representation. In contrast, the American technological sublime is built on a pleasure of a positive kind, for it concerns an apparently successful representation of man's ability to construct an infinite and perfect world. (287)

Where does this lead us? Nye summarizes his lamentation as follows: "In the search for this positive pleasure, a 'consumer's sublime' has emerged as Americans shop for new sensations of empowerment" (ibid.). The Christos provide the shopping malls for these consumers; they are savvy enough to realize that the purchase of their graphic drawings (object art) is no substitute for the sensation of empowerment, a sensation one may feel in the vastness of the West, where nature is inviting and constrained—fenced, covered, wrapped, surrounded (environmental art)—and where anyone is welcome to join in the fabrication of golden calves.

Product, Process, and Politics

As most art critics acknowledge, the focus of attention is on an artistic object, a painting, sculpture, or even a photograph. It is something that draws attention, that begs for an analysis, that expresses in its representational mode something "real." An entire history of art and aesthetics is based on questions of representation or, in more contemporary parlance, referencing. Movements, such as deconstruction and postmod-

ernism, have taken upon themselves to provide theoretical bridges or fill
intellectual gaps in relation to works of art and the culture that surrounds
them. Instead of following their theoretical concerns (translating them, as
they do, into linguistic and analytic structures and functions), we direct
our exploration to specific facets (commercialized technoscience) that
accompany those avant-garde artists in the twentieth century that retain
a critical element in their work. Let us make it clear that what is of utmost
importance is not an underlying linear progression or regression of the
potential for avant-garde art (in either Clement Greenberg's or Arthur
Danto's sense). Rather, we are concerned with the critical dimension of
artworks that expose current ambiguities, and that emphasize the tension
endemic to artworks of the twentieth century (in the face of the powers
of modernity).

As mentioned in chapter 1, Duchamp was able to transform the aesthetic experience from the traditional perception of classical, high-art
objects of contemplation to a paradoxical appreciation of everyday
objects, such as a urinal. Duchamp is still concerned with objects or, in
his case, industrial, mass-produced products. But what makes his concern
relevant to us is that the objects he chooses to be his ready-mades are
themselves mass produced and commercially available technoscientific
products. As such, they point to a whole industrial and commercial
process that brings them into being, that makes them what they are
(including the creative aspect). In a different vein, Magritte likewise still
focuses on objects in his culture and the nature that surrounds them, so
that his innovation is the puzzling juxtaposition of "things out there," as
if to remind his audience that the conventions of their day are as arbitrary
as his choice of juxtaposition. Magritte, like Duchamp, is concerned with
his own artworks as products of an artistic imagination that are made for
gallery and museum consumption (perhaps some art collectors should be
included here, too). All of these consumers, unlike the consumers the
Christos envision, hope to enjoy and even acquire an object of a definite
aesthetic value.

The artistic products themselves are questioned only about their subject matter and the execution of their representation of other objects or
products. As we saw with Klein and Boggs in chapter 2, it is clear that the
focus of some avant-garde artists has moved from product to process, the
long chain of links between the artist and the product sold to someone
else. This process was the highlight of Klein's exchange, since the product to be sold was nothing but Parisian air (or as he called it, "Immater-

ial Zones"). Boggs continues that change in focus by insisting that the so-called artistic product is itself only a partial object of acquisition, and that the gamble or trust one must have in an artistic piece of work is itself an open-ended question. In both cases not only is the process of artistic creation, distribution, and consumption important, but the entire commercial world that surrounds all transactions is foregrounded, as with Boggs's "Art Money."

As all the cultural processes that define the art world become more explicit and publicly discussed, not just those defining moments of curatorial judgment and authority, one necessarily becomes cognizant of the political atmosphere that hinders or encourages transactions that include artworks or that challenge the foundation of capitalist commercial values. Warhol and Haring embodied in their works and lives the collapse of the artificial distinction—perhaps romantic, perhaps religious—between products and processes. For example: "Neither Warhol's working method nor his techniques [the Factory and the photo-silk-screens] were unusual in a successful commercial artist and only the gurus of the idealistic view of art would be shocked by his use of the industrial society's work-sharing system. . . . In order to pass their painting off as an 'original' the Renaissance painters themselves only had to paint the most important parts . . . while they left the rest of the fresco or the picture to their assistants" (Honnef 26). Historically recognized artists from past centuries, such as Rubens and Rodin, perfected this production system and established their own mini-factories or manufacturing facilities. Once factories for art and the business of art take center stage in the world of art, it is no wonder that the public becomes more confused about the valuation of artworks (both old masters and avant-garde). Are they yet another set of objects for consumption? Are they status symbols? Are they the paths to an experience of the sublime? Are they the representation and symbols of the history of art?

Here is where the Christos enter our discussion. The collapse of product and process is obvious in their works, because their attempts at wrapping and unwrapping the world as they choose bespeaks the commercial activity of buying and selling, or defining one's world in terms of the marketplace of commodities. How far this can be extended has been the ruling question of their work as they moved from more modest objects, such as art books and magazines, to larger objects, such as storefronts and small structures (such as the Kunsthalle in Bern, Switzerland). Eventually the enterprise got bigger and bigger, and entire islands were

114 "surrounded"—an idea of Jeanne-Claude's. But what this frequently
◇ required was a series of necessary appeals to political leaders for legal
authorization (permits), property owners for permission to use their land,
buyers to purchase their drawings to finance the projects, and the public
at large for the necessary work force and technical staff. But with all this
in mind, we still believe that the Christos' environmentally awe-inspiring
work is concerned with the sublime as Kant understood it, and that when
they succeed in appealing to large audiences it is because of and not
despite their religious pretensions. In what follows, we shall discuss
aspects of the spiritual longing that remained unsatisfied at the end of the
millennium, thereby reconsidering the main issues of our book.

The Christ(os)

Christo Javacheff (like his wife) uses professionally no full name, only
the one-word label "Christo." When Reuters wants to be more specific in
its description of him, it calls him "the environmental artist," as if by this
label there is a legitimation of his projects—being displayed in or on the
environment. An informative example of one of his projects that traverses
the grounds of religious belief, natural awe, and the politics of self-promotion and avant-garde art may be *The Valley Curtain* of 1970–72. This
project, a temporary wall of fabric spanning an entire mountain valley
near Rifle, Colorado, was certainly art materialized at an unimaginable
scale. Was it a miracle in the making?

The valley curtain collapses the question of the sublime in nature and
its appropriation into a question about the miracle-maker himself. Jesus
never called attention to himself as a producer of miracles; instead, his
miracles were of use to others and pointed to the sublime power of God.
Unlike Christ, Christo draws attention to his own power, the power to
subvert nature, to curtain-off a valley so that the curtain, useless as it is,
becomes the focus of attention. But even Christ, the Son of God, seems
not to be enough for Christo's ambition. Interfering with God's creation
to the extent of putting up a barrier in a valley alludes to his deep-seated
desire to compare himself to the Father. Is Christo indeed an equal part-
ner, co-creator of nature, fellow designer, architect, and artist?

As Dominique Laporte says: "A curtain blocks the valley. Are they
erecting a frontier? An impassable boundary that will force drivers to go
back? The limits of the world defined once and for all, a roadblock com-
mensurate with the human effort to push back the boundaries of the

known world as far as possible and thus to build new roads, new bridges? . . . Is it the priests alone who define the limits of the known world[?] And the warriors who build walls around conquered territories[?] Is this curtain defending a world beyond? Is it a frontier drawn by a new kind of a conqueror?" (53, 55).

Since Christo, like Christ, has an aerial or heavenly view of the environment, and since his presence, through umbrellas or other materials, is only as a prophet or messiah, there is no personal culpability for unfortunate deaths. Lori Rae Mathews—a viewer tragically killed by one of the umbrellas during a windstorm—had to die; this was the price to be paid in human flesh that the gods deemed necessary in order for humans to understand their function here on earth. But whose ideas are being displayed? And why display umbrellas on hillsides, in the U.S. and Japan? Why wrap islands in brightly colored, water-resistant synthetic surfaces? (Bourdon 168–77).

Is Christo a modern incarnation of Jesus Christ (as suggested earlier)? Is he hiding something underneath those colorful wrappings? Is he shielding the earth or the seas from the sun, from the human gaze? In whose name does he work—the name of God? Assume for a minute that Christo is indeed an environmental artist, that is, that he works with nature, on nature, and outside the confines of studios and museums in order to make contemporary culture more sensitive to the environment. Assume that his artistic vision expresses his ideological commitment, and that both bespeak certain ecologically informed values. Now what? Are old-fashioned Christian values, those by which Christo as Christ must live daily, so bankrupt that one needs to concoct new ones, so-called ecologically informed ones? How do the values of the environmental artist fit or displace the values of the Christian or humanist artist? Are we merely pointing our Christian finger at Christo because of his name, his namesake? Can we avoid doing this? Should we?

Christ's vision, as it has been canonically transmitted to us throughout the ages, was undertaken and portrayed with words and promises, using verbal images that eventually found themselves into canvases and marble, into studios and churches, into museums and private collections. The verbal images used by Christ were transitory and transcendental at the same time, so that the flight of thought and vision, the words that only disciples could remember and write down, could not be fastened to a grid, imprisoned, and become petrified. The words as images of Jesus had the impact that no written words could have, because they were uttered with

116   the conviction and flair that are afforded only to gods—or their sons, for
◇   that matter. The inscriptions left behind are relics found in churches and
in people's minds, relics whose significance is the personal investment
individuals make when they regard them as religious, visionary, divine.
Christ's power does not rest with a kingdom on earth, but with his crucifixion and death, his resurrection and frailty, his heavenly existence.

Christo also creates, quite deliberately, temporal pieces (Sonfist 17),
covering natural images such as hillsides and rivers, islands and trees,
with colors, emulating the portrayal of the divine vision of Christ. When
the concrete presence of nature is encountered, Christo takes flight with
his technical apparatus and shifts the language of nature, of matter and
rocks, into the language of colors, transcendence, and heaven. Christo
wants to translate the temporal into the eternal (Sayre 230), just like
Christ, but can he? What does it take for Christo to achieve a Christ-like
status? Is it a crucifixion? Or is it enough to crucify, on the rocks, with the
aid of strong winds and a giant umbrella, a woman? Will her death bring
salvation (or just a news report)?

Christo transcends the particularity of the terrain he covers, for in its
uniformity, the cloth, the strong color, the evenness of the display, its repetition—why 1,760 umbrellas when one should be enough to make the
same statement?—he tries so very hard to speak to us in the language of
timelessness, the spiritual or religious language that defies common
words and idioms, that has a certain universal style of presentation. In his
style of re-presentation, Christo plays with the idea of covering and
revealing, as if nature can be hidden and its secrets protected by painted
fabrics, or revealed and its secrets exposed. Who is Christo to play so
freely with natural artifacts, big as they are, to cover and uncover them,
to maintain a dominion over God's playground?

What Jesus could do in the name of God, Christo tries to do in the
name of capitalism. Capitalism in this context means at the very least the
cult of the genius, the heroic individual who conquers visionary vistas,
who is an entrepreneur at heart, who follows classical American mottoes
and modes of behavior of the rugged individual who scales mountains on
the way to the wild West. The conquest is capitalist in nature because it
is competitive to the core and is done with the explicit goal of acquiring
happiness and glory through profits (gold and silver, for example).

The grand scale of Christo's displays is harnessed by technological
feats that only a great deal of money can bring about (as we learned, the
Umbrellas Project cost $26 million). This is power and dominance, the

power of tools and instruments, of legal contracts and insurance compa-
nies, and not the power of religious visions. Christo tames nature and
alleviates the anxiety of humans about nature by covering it, by mediating
the wilderness experience or the fear of nature by presenting nature all
dressed up, covered, cultured, aesthetically garbed. But why is there a
fear of nature in this Christ/Christo axis of deliverance?

The Christian, biblical Fall is about nakedness, about the shame of
nudity in God's watchful eye and the eyes of a man and a woman. The
Original Sin is simultaneously the sin of lying to God and disobeying His
command and also the sin of seduction and nudity, the sin of desire and
passion. When sensuality is covered, sexuality is hidden, as if it can be
made to disappear. But this is the sensuality of nature and of culture, not
simply that of the human flesh. For in the nudity of the human flesh one
envisions nature and culture, the temporal existence of humans and the
cultural codes inscribed on humans' bodies. Human nudity and the
nudity of nature seem to be one and the same for the Christ/Christo axis,
for they all need to be covered, a cover up operation that can use religious
institutions and doctrine or artistic ones.

But Christo's coverings are not limited to naked reality (understood
naturalistically). When Christo embarks on many of his projects for covering structures, those human artifacts that have dominated our visual
landscape at least since the industrial revolution, he hits upon another
admonition of Jesus'. Following the biblical admonition against vanity—
personal and cultural—Christo covers the Pont Neuf in Paris, for example, and the Reichstag headquarters in Berlin (Bourdon 178–87, 188–97).
The admonition against human folly and vanity is undertaken seriously
already in the Jewish tradition, the artistic expression of which is to be
found in the commandment that stipulates not to make any godlike
graven images—as was so expressly illustrated in the story of the golden
calf. Is Christo following the Jewish tradition of not producing sculptures
and paintings by using the most abstract of all artistic renditions, a cloth?
Is the cloth of many colors to symbolize Joseph in Egypt with his encounters with the pharaoh?

No, Christo seems too Christian to be Jewish at all. His view and critique of contemporary culture are of monumental dimensions, in a truly
Christ-like manner, the manner allotted to saints and gods but not to
mere mortals. When Christo draped the Chicago Museum of Contemporary Art (ibid. 218–45), he was hiding one of the most ostentatious of our
cultural institutions that attempt to claim immortality for human artifacts

118

◇ and by extension to humans. What is an art museum if not a repository for human labor that has gained some prominence and whose claim for immortality is framed and weighed by capitalist yardsticks: how big is it? Or would the issues change if one were wrapping an art history book (as Christo did in 1960)? Which of the two wrappings can be auctioned at Christie's? (Incidentally, the latter was.) What are the implications concerning the history of art? Would Danto's claim about the end of art history be exemplified in this project?

The obsession of encircling the Reichstag with fabric mirrors the Chicago museum project. Just as there is an implicit admonition of human vanity concerning the production, dissemination, and consumption of works of art (one would guess only high art), so there is an implicit desire to admonish the most notorious symbol of ideological (read political, social, and racial) vanity. The Nazi Reich was supposed to last one thousand years; it was supposed to surpass any previous political power known to human history in terms of its military power, geographical expansion, and racial purity. What Christo covered is not the obvious manifestation of an ideological power and vanity gone mad, but the very characterization of history as such. History unfolds as culture and art, as social movements and political parties, as personal idiosyncrasies and collective uniformities; but since historical manifestations are not divine they must remain suspect in the eyes of Christ(o). As such they deserve, whenever their extremes appear, to be hidden, just like the nakedness of nature. But then, of course, the very act of hiding draws attention to the hidden object.

Just as the Fall had an impact on humanity—we covered ourselves so as not to appear naked in public—so does Christo want to have an impact on culture, covering nature and culture so as to hide their "ugly" nakedness in the public eye. Is Christo's cover-up operation a miracle or a personal aggrandization? Does the Christo signature on nature sanctify the earth it touches? Can Christo's fabric floating on the Bay of Biscayne have the same impact as Christ walking on water in the Sea of Galilee? Does Christo have the same impact as the crucified Christ when he wraps himself in "bloody" red cloth (for Annie Leibovitz's celebrity photo portrait)?

Let us return the discussion from the singular to the plural, since there is a much closer and more publicly explicit collaboration between Christo and his wife, Jeanne-Claude. If the parallel between Christ and the Christos holds, it is one whereby an appeal to communal participation and action is made and fulfilled. In both cases, there is enough good will even among skeptics to enable miracles to take place. There is a certain level of passivity that is nonthreatening, because no matter what happens, it will go away, leave you alone, disappear. The temporality of the Christos' projects resemble the burning bush and the parting of the Red Sea. These projects come along infrequently in anyone's lifetime, and then they vanish without leaving discernable traces. The only traces are predetermined products for sale.

It is for the critical aspects of their projects and not for their commercial success that we use the Christos as one of our examples of avant-garde artists working in the twentieth century. Their value both for us (writing this book) and for the culture at large (figuring out what should be done next) is enormous, for they bring to the fore all of the paradoxical conditions under which artworks must be produced, distributed, and consumed today. Their environmental-scale projects may shed some light on the potential for artworks outside commercial (public and private alike) venues available in every major city (and in catalogs as well). What they have done to popularize their ideas goes beyond the museum or gallery shops (though drawings of their projects are always available for sale); they have paralleled the Warhol and Haring phenomena in ways that appeal to wide audiences and could command the attention of popular media (television and documentaries, as well as newspapers). Once again, what makes them avant-garde at all?

> First of all, the community (avant-garde) is categorized by the obliteration of the distinction between high and low culture. . . . Yet the legitimization of popular culture is apparently possible only through its elevation to a religious experience, i.e., the dance [and avant-garde art] cannot be mere fun or entertainment but must, on the contrary, fulfill all the emphatic requirements of bourgeois art. Hesse's utopian redefinition of low culture therefore anticipates the left postmodernist position that claims to discover emancipatory yearnings in the products of the culture industry. (Berman 75)

Perhaps the most that the Christos can hope for in their emergent art of the late twentieth and early twenty-first century is an appeal to human frailty in the face of commercialized technoscience, and the expectations

120
◇
that public experiences of nature and technoscience as transcending the commercialized marketplace (of art, ideas, and commodities) provide the conditions of transcendence.

Perhaps they can finally fulfill the promise made earlier in the twentieth century in relation to the dissemination of artworks and the critical ideals of the artistic community. Perhaps they can relate to Stuart Davis, who had faith in the potential of modern art to be fully public—effective even beyond the venues chosen by Warhol and Haring. Bogart quotes Davis, who said in 1921 that the new modern pictures would have

> nothing in common with the trade of the galleries. They should be sold in stores like newspapers and magazines. That is to say large colored reproductions to sell for 5 or 10 dollars. Black and white would be cheaper of course but the idea is that they would be looked forward to as entertainment by a number of people just like the Saturday Eve. Post and have no holy art about them. It should develop into a business just as painting and engraving was in its big days. Of course the logical thing seems to be their publication in a magazine which increases distribution.
>
> Commercial culture offered new ways to reach an audience by providing new channels of mass dissemination. (233)

The Christos have taken the notion of mass dissemination to commercial and international levels that are embraced by popular media and that could not have been envisioned almost a century ago. They have turned blue-collar work into the labor of artists, and vice versa; they have invited every worker to be both an artist and an art critic; they have understood Warhol's and Haring's works to be a beginning and not the end of the popularization of artworks in contemporary culture, becoming as they were in their time celebrities and tele-evangelists for the (aesthetic) sublime.

5

Theory out of Practice

It is the providence of art to set the true ideal that is as
essential for human survival as daily doses of Wonder Bread.

—Cicotello and Sassower, with apologies to William Morris

What Makes Art What It Is?

THERE IS a double meaning to the title of this chapter. On the one
hand, it means that one's theory ought to emerge out of particular
practices, that there is a (Marxian) primacy of practice to theory, that the
former gives rise to the latter. On the other hand, it may also mean that
the theories we use are out of practice, that they are outdated by the time
anyone tries to make use of them. There is no practice that cannot be the-
orized, and there can be no theory that cannot be practiced or illustrated.
In either case, we suggest a critical evaluation of the meaning and usefulness of theoretical treatises when one works with the history of art, art
criticism, and the artistic community in general. We also believe that in
order to judge anything artistic, in order to render judgment about particular practices, one must reveal or articulate the theoretical scaffolding
that props up one's judgment.

Thierry de Duve suggests that the difference between an art historian
and an avant-garde art historian is that the former knows what to write
about, what the facts of the matter are, so to speak, while the historian of
avant-garde art is in the more precarious position of having to judge what
would count as the domain of reference to begin with: "As for the historian of art, art for you is a given domain of facts. As for the historian of the
avant-garde, art for you is a conflict whose outcome is at stake. But more
clearly than most historians of art, you state and take on your responsi-
bilities as judge" (38).

These statements should alert the reader to the inherent problems

122　facing the critic of the avant-garde whose very choices of what to count
◇　as art are themselves open to criticism. So, unlike the Kantian matrix of
the critique of judgment (of aesthetic experiences and the sublime), post-
Duchamp in de Duve's sense of avant-garde aesthetics, there is a more
fundamental matrix that encompasses and overshadows the Kantian one,
namely, the matrix of what counts as art at all. And when one includes
certain works as art, one's judgment comes under scrutiny, even attack.
De Duve continues: "True, as a critic who goes public with his or her preferences, you will be judged on your judgments" (47).

With this in mind, an analysis of one of the major critics of art seems
appropriate for our consideration of the role of theory in contemporary
culture. When Arthur Danto theorizes about the end of art at the end of
the twentieth century, what he means by it (or what his scaffolding tries
to establish) is that "the history of art in the West has been the history of
achieving self-consciousness of the nature of art—of achieving, if you
like, a philosophical understanding of what art is. . . . This was widened
in the early years of this century in the investigations by such figures as
Duchamp—especially by Duchamp. And it culminated in the advanced
art of the 1960s and the 1970s. A great narrative ended in 1964 in the work
of Warhol in particular" (1994, 12–13).

What narrative has ended? What grand narrative, as the French
would call it (in Lyotard's sense), has been completed? As far as Danto is
concerned, this is what we find at the end of the twentieth century: "My
sense is that the faith in art as a primary means and agency of spiritual
transformation has almost totally vanished, and that this explains the van-
ishing of art movements as such. Art today is pretty much just art. The
winds that stirred the waters into waves were those of higher promises
and almost religious assurances" (ibid. 172).

Danto argues that the history of art was predominantly concerned
with an accurate mapping of human perception, and that through that
mapping a great deal more was expected—perhaps a greater vision, perhaps a level of transcendence that would match that of religious experiences. Though Danto does not make direct reference to the story of the
golden calf, it may be relevant here in terms of the accomplice-role that
artists may inadvertently play when the public wishes to escape from daily
chores and the routine of work. But as the history of art progressed into
the twentieth century, the medium itself (art) became the object of study
and scrutiny, so that by the end of the century, and with the advance of
modernism, art was "driven by philosophical theories regarding the nature

of art, and negation played a central role in this history since so much of it consists of refutation" (ibid. 205).

If art as we used to know it no longer provides a progressive history that leads to an eventual transcendence, and if art is condemned to being self-critical, then what is left of that part of our culture we call art? What does it mean to say, as Danto does, that "art is just art," or that anything can be construed as art? What happens to criteria of judgments and to judgments themselves? "In general," Danto suggests, "something receives that status [art] when some segment of the art world prevails, and objects in question become occasions for appreciation and interpretation of a kind that has no application to things that are not works of art." It is, in short, an act of "enfranchising maneuver" dictated by "curators, art writers, collectors, dealers, and, of course, artists themselves" (ibid. 312).

If there is anything postmodern in this definition, it is the sense of self-legitimation so clearly announced in Lyotard's classification and explanation of the postmodern condition. The plasticity of the definition of art, or the elasticity with which one expands the net in which artworks can find their home, has its limits, argues Danto. But these limits themselves are designed and set in place by that segment of the art world that has the power to dictate what does and what does not count as art. The good news is that the barriers to the artistic world have been lowered; the bad news is that the gatekeepers still have the ultimate power to deny access to whomever they dislike. Perhaps the worthy news is the acknowledgment that commercialized technoscience remains the mainstay for anyone wishing to appeal to the public and sell their wares in the marketplace of ideas, objects, and entertainment.

One hears in Danto's description of his theory of art a Benjamin-like lament over the loss of the potential for transcendence. One hears in this lament a sadness that there is only art to be found in art, and nothing more, as if one had been promised that something greater and better would accompany anything deemed artistic or having aesthetic value. But Danto himself is not so keen on admitting his yearning for the spiritual validation that art could command and supply, though he does admit his debt to Hegel and to the Hegelian sense of beauty or aesthetic value. He terms his own theory pluralist, and claims from his pluralist perspective that the self-consciousness of contemporary works of art demands the ability to comprehend and encompass all the works of art that are available in an age and a culture.

In this context, it may be useful to quote from de Duve in relation to

124 the Hegelian influence over the views of avant-garde art in the twentieth
◇   century: "If, since Mallarmé, the ideology of the avant-garde has been
massively Hegelian, this is because the end of modernity, the end of the
idea of art as proper name, its completion through incompletion, has been
the program ever since Hegel's *Vorlesungen über die Aesthetik*. With
Hegel, the object of aesthetics is no longer the beautiful or taste; it is art
in its autonomy. It is also art in its historical destiny, the necessary alienation that accompanies its 'progress,' and the object of its disappearance"
(77). The predicaments of modernity, as we alluded to them already in the
Introduction, receive another form of public attention when the subject
of art and its constitutive objects comes under discussion. The Hegelian
dimension of the current debate is worth mentioning because it reminds
us of the potential for an *Aufhebung,* a movement toward a new intellectual if not actual plateau, where conflicting ideas and practices may find
temporary relief, even reconciliation. Yet, the potential for reconciliation,
as de Duve reminds us, may turn out to be the dada moment "when the
prohibition and its transgression flow together into their contrary: it is
permitted to do whatever, let's do it" (333). The dada moment may turn
out to be nihilistic from the perspective of traditional art history and the
classical definitions of art, but it also may turn out to be a moment for celebration, when new opportunities arise for those interested in art and the
aesthetic experience.

Danto contrasts his pluralistic theory with that of Clement Greenberg, a purist whose argument for self-definition in the artwork demands
the single pursuit of pure forms in art (and more specifically in modernist
paintings; Danto 1994, 326–27). It is worthwhile pursuing Danto's line of
thought, for it illustrates the confusion over the designation of certain
objects as artworks. The confusion itself is symptomatic of an age of confusion that insists on definitions, on clarity of thought, and on precise
classifications. Only against the background of great upheavals, of terri-
ble strife and human devastation, does it make sense to call for purity of
language and thought.

Natural languages (as opposed to artificial languages) are by definition complex and beyond simple reduction, and it is no wonder that the
cultures that emanate from them or that use them also are complex. But
what remains at the end of the day is the judgment we make of these complexities: they are not frightening sights we must simplify and systematize
(as Freud and Jung do with the dream world), but causes for celebration
because of the richness of experiences and the open-endedness they allow

human intelligence and emotions. Here we part ways with most critics of the late twentieth century in America.

Moreover, we believe that nothing can withstand the power of capitalism, art included. This is the case not so much because of the monolithic nature of that power, but rather because of its elasticity and adaptability. The systems created by capitalism are lasting because of the incessant concern to incorporate into them all that there is: nature, humanity, and the space that exists between them. Even religious aspirations are for the most part bought and sold in the marketplace, where cathedrals are built and where dues are collected. Missionary work is enhanced or retarded by the ability of church institutions to raise the funds to support ideals. The art world or the community of artists cannot resist or subvert this reality or the systems that have been woven within it.

If indeed the art world cannot resist its incorporation into the capitalist system, then one must pay critical attention to the nature of that incorporation. Must the art world agree with the principles of greed and profitability? Who will finance its proliferation? If popes and princes have become obsolete, then must the new bourgeoisie take over the patronage of the arts? If they do so, will they accept artistic criticism that mocks their accomplishments? In some sense, this is already the case, since there is a psychosocial predisposition to appreciate the predicament of the arts and the position into which artists are put when they are asked to express the glory of their culture while maintaining a critical distance from it. As Oskar Bätschmann explains, the public feels more qualified to judge works of art than scientific claims because they are "designed for effect, and feelings are common to all" (55). If this is indeed the case, then the artistic community can make claims for closer affinity with the public, and thereby circumvent the hierarchy of state and church patronage. But, as Bätschmann argues, "The demand for artistic freedom in the form of independence of state institutions and patrons necessitated claiming the status of genius" (67).

But what does the designation "genius" entail? According to Bätschmann, "The genius, who always has a wild element in him, breaks the rules and the laws in order to reach the sublime. . . . he changes the world. . . . The genius is in advance of his time. . . . This was also the basis of one view of the avant-garde in art" (ibid.). This sense of freedom through the claim for genuine creativity provided Honore de Balzac in 1830 with an

126 explanation of the widening gap between the genius artist and the public
◇ at large. In addition, this explanatory model also incorporated a view of
the messianic quality of artistic creation, where the sacrifice of the artist
as martyr was compared to that of biblical prophets, if not Jesus himself
(ibid. 71). Finally, one can conclude that this model provides an accurate
depiction of the artist as a spiritual saint, martyred by bourgeois, philis-
tine indifference, typical of many nineteenth-century avant-garde conceptions (see Gauguin's self-portraits).

By the late eighteenth century and the middle of the nineteenth century two contradictory models emerge in regard to the role artists play in
modern society. The despotism of monarchies, benign or malevolent, has
been replaced by the reign of democracies, with their new constitutions
and market forces. Appealing to the arts under changed conditions has
been a new experience for the art community itself and for its intellectual
critics. On the one hand, the alienated genius artist was held outside the
daily turmoil and regarded as a transcendent voice whose spiritual appeal
could be discovered in the future. On the other hand, the artist with a
keen and critical eye, with an imaginative vision, could be a useful instrument in the hands of reformists and revolutionary political, social, and
moral forces. Which role will the artist choose, if a choice is even an
option?

According to Friedrich Schiller, at the end of the eighteenth century
art could be the reconciling force between the harsh realities of nature
and its constraints on humanity, and the moral aspirations of newly
formed societies. Art could be useful for the education of the masses, a
way of appealing to an audience wider than the one reached through the
channels of a legal code or system of laws. But in order to be in forefront
of society, in order to further the progress of the political agenda of
democracy, artists themselves had to be placed beyond any suspicion of
corruption, following political reason and their own liberty. As
Bätschmann explains about this particular period of European history:
"the idea of an avant-garde in the arts was developed not by artists but by
the imaginary figure of the artist in the Saint-Simon movement. The idea
is not based on an analysis of the arts but on the concern to incorporate
artists in a system that judged activities according to their usefulness—
'utilité'—for social development. It is ironic that the term 'avant-garde'
was first used for artists when the need was felt to accord the arts a function in the global industrial system and make them propagators for the

general good" (ibid. 74). And here is the rub: while artists seem no more than the propagators of the common good, as it is currently defined by the powers to be, they are also expected to use their creative genius to anticipate the future and thereby transcend the conditions that give rise to their work. Their predicament, and the attendant public confusion, seems therefore quite reasonable, even common-sense. Could one combine these two roles, these two tendencies found in the artistic community? As far as Laverdant was concerned in 1845, one could do both: "Art is the expression of a society, and at its peak it represents the most progressive social tendencies; it is both prophecy and revelation. To discover whether art can credibly fulfil its pioneering task, whether an artist is really in the avantgarde, one naturally has to know whither mankind is heading, what his destiny is" (ibid.).

But when the avant-garde is accorded its role as both prophetic and revealing, when it claims usefulness in the service of lofty goals while admonishing the public for failing to follow the most progressive of social, political, and moral tendencies, when it claims to be the judge and critic of the culture in which it works, then it sets itself up to be rejected as well. As José Ortega y Gasset claimed in 1925, "The new art has the mass against it, and always will have" (ibid. 180). This is the case because of a deep-felt alienation between what the avant-garde produces and what the public perceives and understands. And the minute there is a split among those who claim to understand the meaning of avant-garde art or contemporary art, the minute there is a split among the public, a growing hostility will develop toward artists and their work. Besides, visual art, which is supposedly the most accessible to cultural expressions, has almost been hijacked by critics and historians in the last century as the exclusive instrument of critical evaluation the gist of which only the privileged can appreciate. What was historically the most popular and audience-friendly cultural expression has turned into an elitist activity only the initiated can comprehend.

The hostility toward the rich and powerful is easily diverted to those who are perceived to be their protectors and accomplices—artists. Twenty years after Gasset, Robert Motherwell reiterates some of these sentiments, trying to explain the break and hostility that characterize the relationship between the public and the art world. As far as Motherwell is concerned, what brought artists and their audiences together during medieval times was the affinity with and appreciation of religious relics,

128 icons, and artistic expressions. By modern times, there had developed a
◇   gap between the subjects and objects the public and artists are interested
in. The Catholic Church no longer holds the reins on the culture as a
whole (ibid. 190).

It wasn't until later in the twentieth century that it became clear how
divorced modern art was from its immediate environments. Rather than
express a particular political aim, and thereby be accused of being propa-
gandists—and if this is true, the employees of fascism as well as democracy—artists wanted to retain a separation and prophetic power that
could transcend the cultural constraints of their time (that is, they are
beholden neither to pope nor princes). When they did that, they were
accused of being aloof and beyond comprehension. Either way, then, they
could be condemned. How could they hope to redeem themselves or be
active participants in their cultures? How can they hope to achieve some
level of transcendence without thereby alienating themselves from their
surroundings (as Nye so aptly noticed in the case of the transformation of
the conception of the sublime)? How can they hope, in Poggioli's terms,
to "not only [destroy] the barbed-wire of rules, the gilded cage of classical poetics, but also [create] a new morphology of art, a new spiritual language?" (57).

The quest for transcendence in and of itself is not misguided, but the
means may need to change radically, or our expectations for achieving the
quest must be transformed. So, the issue at hand is not so much the definition of art or of avant-garde art, but the context in which avant-garde
art can flourish. The lament regarding modern art expressed by Benjamin
or Gasset could turn into a postmodern celebration. But the question
remains, what is the lament all about? Is the lament over the transformation of the role of avant-garde art as the socially emancipatory force
expected by its critics and promoters? Is it over the loss of the possibility
of art to provide spiritual deliverance? Or is it regret about losing the centrality of artworks as cultural ornamentations that were part of state and
church alike? Has mechanical reproduction of works of art, especially
film, overwhelmed the possibility of artworks as conduits of sublime experiences?

The survival of art, and the art world, will depend not on its prophetic
mission nor on its expression of the latest and most progressive political
agenda. Rather, its survival will depend on the avant-garde exploration of
and immersion in the commercialized technoscientific world. In this

transformation what becomes apparent is the shift from a notion of beauty and the sublime as a special sensitivity and legitimation of the elite to the insistence on public accessibility to critically examine daily experiences and now call them culture. In this respect, then, the yearning for the sublime depends on (rather than ignores or circumvents) the innovations of commercialized technoscience. Avant-garde art participates in these innovations so as to reach some level of transcendence, but it does so without seeking an idealist refuge.

The liberation of the art world from the shackles of the church and the monarchy seemed an attractive solution for the creative artist, until it was realized that freedom alone could not pay the bills. One could return to the church, appeal to the new aristocracy, or plead with political institutions, all of which were perceived as restricting the cult of the genius. The last alternative was complete autonomy with the prospect of selling one's work on the open market. But, as Bätschmann so carefully documents, there are numerous obstacles to such aspiration. How does one get public notice? How does one arrange for one's works to be displayed? And, unlike in previous ages when commissions were prearranged, the artist must now work first in a speculative mode, investing in materials and marketing the work, and only later expect to be paid. As of the late eighteenth century artists became part of the world of commerce without intending to be so; as of the late twentieth century artists became more openly integrated into the world of commerce, creating their own standards of aesthetic value and financial rewards.

The price for artistic autonomy is dependency on financial power. In the past financial dependence has been understood and exercised through personal indebtedness (to a pope or a queen). In modern times, this dependence has been exchanged for impersonal debts to national endowments, academic institutions, and at times the marketplace of artistic exchange, where gallery and museum curators and directors control the value of aesthetic pleasures. In contemporary culture one could claim a certain liberation from the personal shackles that tied artists to a particular town or region; now they are free to venture internationally and accept commissions across the globe. But this also means that once the commerce of reproduction made some artists famous in the public's eye, they could no longer be shielded by the elite surroundings of wealthy collectors and museum curators—they have become fully exposed. They live in a fishbowl that is on display on television screens and in daily tabloids.

130 Perhaps the history of American commercial art in the twentieth century
◇ tells more clearly the story of artistic freedom and the constraints of economic conditions that determine the development of avant-garde culture.

Commercializing Art

A nineteenth-century myth about the separation between fine and
commercial art, or between high and low art, set the tone for the history
of art in the twentieth century. This myth dates back to the Renaissance
era, when painters and sculptors elevated themselves above the rest of the
artisans into a guild equal to the liberal arts guilds. What has helped
maintain this myth is the emergence of the Enlightenment ideals that
focused on liberty and equality. The parallel was drawn between freedom
and the fine arts (where inspiration and spiritual transcendence or the
sublime are offered as salvation from the daily chores of commerce) and
bondage and the commercial arts (where the design and manufacturing of
consumable objects is dictated by the marketplace and price pressure).
The myth, then, is about the potential for preserving the fine arts in an
elevated position within the cultural matrices that in the twentieth century are supposed to be wholly capitalistic.

This myth of the privileged status of fine arts first came under attack
during the middle of the nineteenth century, when photographers cam-
paigned for the inclusion of their product, their craft, their art, in the official exhibitions of fine art. In the late nineteenth century, the aesthetic
theory of William Morris's arts and crafts ideal argued for the abolishment
of what Morris considered both a false and, more important, immoral distinction between the so-called fine and commercial arts (Thompson
253–56). Michele Bogart provides an excellent overview of the nascent
acceptance and eventual rejection of the favored status of fine art by
focusing on American commercial art in the twentieth century. According
to her: "Throughout the first half of the century, artists strove to relate
purposefully to the corporate presence, to explore possibilities offered by
new media and centers of cultural power. . . . adjustment to the new mar-
ket-oriented frameworks presented technical, aesthetic, and professional
challenges. Romantic ideals remained a persistent influence on image
production and artistic identity" (301).

Bogart notes the ambivalence that permeated the art world during the
first half of the twentieth century in relation to the commercialization of
artists' works and the ongoing temptation to be more rather than less

involved with the business world (256–57). This temptation was acted upon more often than not, and there was a certain belief that the old myth of the freedom that comes with fine arts was being replaced by the myth that freedom comes with commercial success.

According to Bogart: "Like illustration, the advertising poster was widely regarded as an exciting new art form at the turn of the century. In the view of many artists, writers, and businessmen, good posters would oil the machinery of economic progress; the harmonious conjunction of art and commerce would also help society to reach its fullest potential." Historically speaking, then, "in the late 1930s and early 1940s, collaborations between unusual clients and art directors, painters and graphic designers led to speculations that fine art and commercial art were converging" (79, 4).

Instead of replacing one outdated myth with another, equally inapplicable myth, one can reconfigure the relationship between fine and commercial art (if one is determined to hold on to this distinction in the first place). For instance, one could argue that preserving the myth of the privileged position of fine arts could help elevate not only fine arts as such but all the other facets and dimensions of creative activity, that is, add legitimacy to the very production of aesthetically appealing objects and products, no matter who the artist happens to be. Following is a wonderful example of the concern with artistic status and the commercial setting in which it comes under attack. Note the comments on the contract signed by Georgia O'Keeffe with Hawaiian Pineapple. To quote Bogart:

> Even great modern artists like O'Keeffe were not so different from everybody else. Even they would "stoop" to commerce. This, and the fact that their advertisements worked, were proof that art and advertising were perfectly compatible. Yet precisely because art could contribute so much to advertising, advertisers should cultivate art and especially excellence in art as something special and important. Art created by painters like Georgia O'Keeffe was different from run-of-the mill commercial imagery. Coiner and his creative staff had proved as much. Advertisers should thus listen to art directors like himself and take their art expertise seriously. . . .
>
> The advertisements that [Coiner] and his staff commissioned worked not only because they were good and unusual art and design, but also because they were pitched to an audience that was conscious of the status value attributed to cultivated high

modernism. This emphasis on the prestige of modern art—made by Artists—diverged from the ideal of integrated professional practice envisioned by Pousette-Dart and Bauhaus theoreticians. (166, 168)

Morris's proposals of integrating the different facets of art within his arts and crafts ideal were taken up by the Bauhaus practitioners so as to prove the interconnectedness between theory and practice or between arts and crafts (so that the machine—with its inherent aesthetic value— would be the ultimate tool and goal of integration). As Bogart insists, though, integration is a more complex undertaking than merely designating one group of artists as different from or the same as another group of artists. The minute commerce and technoscience enter the cultural equation, a power struggle emerges (and here the echo of Marx's lament sounds frightfully real when Morris repeats it in the context of aesthetics, a context supposedly shielded from the ugliness of labor strife and class struggle). As Bogart explains:

> The changing boundaries of fine and commercial art resulted from efforts on the part of painters, illustrators, advertisers, advertising artists, art directors, photographers, and assorted elite groups to claim jurisdiction over "art" as a means of acquiring authority and influence in their fields and in the broader culture. A great deal was at stake for all involved. . . . Power was a crucial variable. Three issues in particular help to highlight these changing relations of authority: the tension between romantic ideals and commercial activity; the vacillating attitudes toward art's relation to commodities; and changing interpretations of the relationship of art and audience. (7)

Looking at the post–World War II American experience with commercialized technoscience and the arts, Bogart marks the period in this manner: "with the emergence of television, the terrain of art practice expanded and became more stratified, but the ideological borders of fine art narrowed and rigified" (4). How did this formulate itself in light of earlier attempts to merge the fine and commercial arts? Bogart answers: "The 1950s marked a period of notable reconfiguration in which romantic high-art values, privileging autonomous creation and reception, emerged triumphant. The shift in emphasis from occupational to aesthetic debate signaled a resolution of the question regarding the borders of art: 'Fine' art was clearly separate from other artistic enterprises. The shift was manifest in the rising interest in contemporary American painting and the explosion of its market value" (301).

The resolution Bogart discusses was only temporary, since immediately after that period (avant-garde) Pop Art (see Warhol and Haring) and the "democratic" Action Art of Joseph Beuys deliberately blurred all previously agreed upon lines of demarcation. The explosion of market value is correct, since right after the war prices of artworks jumped by at least two decimal points. This explosion in price (and not necessarily in aesthetic value) could come about only because there was an explosion in the financial markets as well. The prosperity of the postwar era allowed for additional disposable income that could be used for commodities other than food, shelter, and clothing. For example, the GI Bill brought higher education to the general public almost as if the tenet of the Enlightenment were guiding the political leadership of the United States. Government was perceived less as a police force than as a mediator and empowering force to ensure public freedom and equality (progressive taxation, free education, and mortgages for all).

In this context, it is interesting to recall something different from the control of art prices, namely, the control of their display. When it came to government regulation of posters and billboards, of advertising of any artistic kind, the courts (in the 1910s) claimed that "aesthetics were a 'matter of luxury and indulgence rather than of necessity, and it is necessity alone which justifies the exercise of police power'" (ibid. 97). Incidentally, one could perceive Keith Haring's subway drawings as being a late reflection on this debate, and an exposition on the very spaces where art can or should be publicly shown or consumed (as discussed in chapter 3).

If art is a matter of luxury and personal taste, and if artists should remain aloof from the tensions of the marketplace, does this mean that the arts should not be part of the government push toward greater integration and social support for liberty and equality? Bogart explains that the American commitment to individualism in the face of government support is no different from the artistic commitment to individualism (creativity, originality, genius) in the face of commercial support (commissions by industrial corporations). In this context we should remember that the eighteenth-century avant-garde held on to this ideal of progressive art as intellectual and spiritual salvation (as did its Enlightenment

134
◇

counterparts). In Bogart's words: "Recognition of the pervasiveness of ide-
ologies of artistic freedom and individualism will help to explain how, on
one level at least, business and commercial interests succeeded in claiming jurisdiction over art, and why debates about art were initially central
to the production and process of advertising and later marginal to them"
(13).

It is of interest that in the Bauhaus, foundations course books relat-
ing to American entrepreneurial genius Henry Ford (creative, innovative,
efficient, socially concerned, and productive) were assigned readings.
Moreover, as Bogart says, "The modernism question forced art directors
to probe the relationship between art and authenticity, raising issues of
aesthetics and ethics that—despite the assertions of some advertising
men—were essential to the advertising process. Similar concerns about
art, advertising, and values were implicit in concurrent discussions
regarding the artist's signature" (143).

So, individualism or authenticity will haunt those who wish to make
a living from their trade. Just as technoscientific innovations are patented
and then used for a fee, so there is a sense that any work of art that is
reproduced, as a poster or as commercial art, should retain its status as
fine art despite its mechanical reproduction. But, unlike with technoscientific patents that are meant to be reproduced and widely marketed, one
remains suspicious of the reproductions of the Mona Lisa—the one with
Duchamp's added moustache, for example. Can one really claim a sense
of ownership of a Ford that is equivalent to that of the Mona Lisa? The
Ford is one of many, the Mona Lisa just one. Yet, many Americans are as
proud of their Fords as the Louvre's curator is of the one and only Mona
Lisa—they belong to them, and they can do with them whatever they
wish! For example, the way some owners transform their Fords into "low
riders" shows how authenticity and even signature come into play even in
mass-produced objects.

By the time we reach Warhol, Haring, or the Christos, Bogart would
admit that "What linked all of these artists by the 1960s, however, was the
fame they had as a result of mass reproduction of their images. By juxta-
posing his own art and the Old Master pictures, [Norman] Rockwell
asserted that the relationship between fine art painting and commercial
culture was an intimate one, integral to the identity of any famous and
popular artistic practitioner of the twentieth century" (3).

Bogart's recollection of similar debates over the past century in relation to commercial art in the U.S. parallels our own concern with avant-

garde art and the reality of commercialized technoscience. Her examples
are poignant, her illustrations are striking, and her analysis lucid and con-
cise. We agree with her assessment of the interlocked positions undertaken by different art directors, artists, and general managers of large corporations who controlled commercial art in the U.S. As we illustrated
with Klein and Boggs (in chapter 2), the role of value—financial and artistic alike—comes under different scrutiny by the middle of the twentieth
century: capitalism has become so much more pervasive than ever before,
and its support of technoscientific dominance over contemporary culture
is primarily lauded and encouraged by the media it controls. Critical
voices are overshadowed and relegated to academic institutions and
poorly distributed print media.

An on-again, off-again relation, a love-hate fest experienced by generation after generation of artists and their corporate benefactors, is illustrated well by what fine-art painter Nathaniel Pousette-Dart (quoted in
Bogart) said in the early 1920s: "Many artists feel that commercial art is a
bad influence on their more serious work. I believe this view erroneous.
Commercial Art, properly approached, can improve, rather than injure,
the ability to create pure art. A man's art can only be as great as he is himself. If his commercial art helps him to broaden and deepen, his pure art
should benefit" (149).

The benefit of commercial art to fine art blurs the distinction
between the two; it also suggests that maintaining this distinction
becomes an anachronism not worthy of contemporary culture's pretense
to be postmodern if not fully modern. Our cursory review of some artworks by Duchamp and Magritte, for example, demonstrates the inter-
locking of fine and commercial creative urges: bottle labels, car ads, mod-
ified graphic art. Of course, Warhol and Haring in their own ways push
the tension to its logical breaking point and bring some sort of cohesion
to the so-called tension or conflict between fine and commercial—or
between low and high—art.

Bogart emphasizes this point with a quote from Edward Steichen, the
eminent photographer of the early twentieth century:

> Indeed, Steichen suggested, any artist working on commission
> was really a commercial artist. Even though the Old Masters
> were like advertising artists, insofar as neither group of artists
> were entirely free and independent. "There has never been a
> period that the best thing we had was not commercial art. If there

136
◇

ever was a poor harassed artist, more so than Michelangelo," he mused tongue-in-cheek, "I never heard of him, thrown on this kind of work and never being able to do what he thought he wanted to do with himself." So much for the romantic myth of the isolated, autonomous fine artist. (183)

Where Do We Go from Here?

As we noted in the Introduction, we are worried neither about personal escapism through aesthetic experiences—what some would term nostalgia in art—nor about the divergence of anecdotes individuals will publicly share—or what some would claim to be the end of the history of art. Instead, we believe that whatever art is to some members of society and however it is classified (for example, as "just art"), it remains a critical endeavor open to individual and group interpretation. We should also note that the discussion of the avant-garde as deserving of elimination (because of its cultural emptiness and social marginality) or celebrity status (because of the high prices commanded for some artworks or the outrageous behavior of some artists) too often misses the point of the heart-wrenching position into which a group of artists are thrust, both as the custodians of eternal values and profound convictions as well as the champions of radical thought and intellectual defiance (against the church and the state alike).

This does not mean that artists, avant-garde or not, should be placed in a preferred position and play an unusual role in their culture. Rather, whatever role they happen to play, whether they express their own whims or visions or portray the ideals of their employers (politicians and corporate leaders alike), they are always open to critical evaluation by themselves and others. The opening of a critical debate is what is at issue for us: the opportunity to reassess that which is taken for granted, the invitation to discuss and debate that which may remain implicit or dormant. The role of artists as public servants, as mediators, and as translators of ideas and theories into practice and objects is one that should be supported if not by government decree then by individual and group generosity (as has been the case with all of the artists we have mentioned in this book).

To retain the myth of artistic creativity and genius as a myth of individualism, freedom, and equality without acknowledging the high price that this myth must command is simply a folly of contemporary society.

For the culture to maintain this myth, it must recognize the commercial and technoscientific matrices that allow it to thrive, or even to survive. Only within the great luxury and wealth of contemporary culture can we uphold such a costly myth; when a nation is robbed of its financial well-being, its culture withers as well. We are not therefore the champions of capitalism and the accumulation of wealth, since wealth can be distributed differently from the ideals of classical capitalism. Yet, we are aware of the linkage that individualism brings about, and the relief that is accorded to the artistic community when it is appreciated by its own society.

We may not break new ground on the final definition of avant-garde art or the exact conditions under which it may develop. Our intent is more modest than that, because we do not believe that one could ever provide a final definition of anything that has cultural interest and life of its own. Instead, we have limited our observations to particular instances where avant-garde claims have been made, and where interesting and critical issues have been raised in the face of artworks. Explaining these issues and interpreting these works within commercialized technoscience could offer a culture a useful method of understanding itself against a background too complex and in flux to be captured with a label or a definition. Ask yourself: What aesthetic experience has made a difference in your life? What artwork have you seen lately that made you blink and think? Where did you see it, and why? Would you recommend it to a friend? The minute you begin answering these questions, you have become a critical observer.

To some extent, this book may be following "the need for new genealogies of the avant-garde, ones that both complicate its past and pluralize its present," as suggested by Hal Foster, whose critique of the Marxian (read Peter Bürger's) dismissal of and lament over the lost critical dimension of avant-garde art since the post–World War II era sets the tone for contemporary discussions of the present status and future prospects of the avant-garde. Foster's critique of Bürger is as follows: as far as Bürger is concerned, the current displays of the avant-garde are nothing but farce and cynical self-obsession—and therefore Bürger's dismissal of the critical potential of the avant-garde seems definitive. Foster objects to Bürger's and Habermas's arguments about the "nonsense experiment" that characterizes the avant-garde, their reluctance to find any meaningful features or critical dimensions to more recent avant-garde works. He insists that there is indeed a critical potential and viability in the continuation of avant-garde works (see Buskirk and Nixon, 5–32). We

138

◇

may not follow Foster's path completely, but we concur that avant-garde artists have played and still play an important critical role.

The fact that we insist on the combination of two cultural phenomena, commerce and technoscience, is what distinguishes our work from those of others. Some books, such as Richard Rush's *Art as an Investment*, Ulrike Klein's *The Business of Art Unveiled*, and Alan Jones and Laura de Coppet's *The Art Dealers*, focus primarily on the economics of the art world. Others, such as Ezra Pound's *Machine Art and Other Writings*, the Museum of Modern Art's *Machine Art* of 1934, and Roger Shattuck's *The Innocent Eye*, focus on the technical, formal, or scientific aspects of the art world. We try to weave a more complex web that combines these two cultural matrices into a critique of artworks; the community of artists, dealers, curators, collectors, and audiences; and the conditions under which artworks are produced, distributed, and consumed.

Our title—*The Golden Avant-Garde*—alludes to the biblical story of the Israelites' impatience with Moses when he went up Mount Sinai to bring down the Ten Commandments. But this title also alludes to the postmodern encounters with commercialized technoscience in general. As Sherrie Levine fabricated her golden replica of Duchamp's *Fountain*, she followed a three-stage process described by de Duve. She first made her choice, a selection, a judgment, of what was worthy to consider as the object of her work; she then inscribed it, in this case in gold; and she signed it, lending it her personal touch, her claim and proof of authenticity. Levine is part of the Duchampian avant-garde response to the age of modernity, a response that remains dialectical (because it is not final) and that invites yet another response, another fabrication. If there is hope and promise in this trajectory of artworks, it is the ongoing engagement and encounters with a changing and challenging culture whose demise or progress can only be judged when it is too late to do anything about it.

Selected Bibliography

Adams, Brooks. "Artist's Chronicle," *Art in America* 84 (October 1996):10, 35, 37.

Adorno, Theodor W. *The Jargon of Authenticity.* Evanston, IL: Northwestern University Press, 1973.

Alloway, Lawrence. *Topics in American Art since 1945.* New York: W. W. Norton, 1975.

Baal-Teshuva, Jacob. *Christo and Jean-Claude.* Cologne: Benedikt Taschen, 1995.

Bätschmann, Oskar. *The Artist in the Modern World: The Conflict between Market and Self-Expression.* Cologne: DuMont Buchverlag, 1997.

Baudrillard, Jean. *America.* New York: Verso, 1988.

———. *For a Critique of the Political Economy of the Sign.* St. Louis, MO: Telos Press, 1981.

Becker, Carol, ed. *The Subversive Imagination: Artists, Society, and Social Responsibility.* New York: Routledge, 1994.

———. *Zones of Contention: Essays on Art, Institutions, Gender, and Anxiety.* Albany: State University of New York Press, 1996.

Benjamin, Walter. "The Work of Art in the Age of Mechanical Reproduction." In *Illuminations.* New York: Schocken, 1969.

Berger, John. *Ways of Seeing.* London: British Broadcasting Corp. and Penguin Books, 1972.

Berman, Russell A. *Modern Culture and Critical Theory.* Madison: University of Wisconsin Press, 1989.

Bockris, Victor. *The Life and Death of Andy Warhol.* New York: Bantam, 1990.

Bogart, Michele H. *Artists, Advertising, and the Borders of Art.* Chicago: University of Chicago Press, 1995.

Bourdon, David. *Christo.* New York: Harry Abrams, 1971.

Buber, Martin. *I and Thou.* Trans. Walter Kaufmann. New York: Charles Scribner's Sons, 1970.

Bürger, Peter. *Theory of the Avant-Garde.* Minneapolis: University of Minnesota Press, 1984.

Buskirk, Martha, and Mignon Nixon, eds. *The Duchamp Effect: Essays, Interviews, Round Table.* Cambridge: MIT Press, 1996.

Butler, Christopher. *After the Wake: An Essay on the Contemporary Avant-Garde.* Oxford: Clarendon Press, 1980.

Cabanne, Pierre. *The Documents of Twentieth-Century Art: Dialogues with Marcel Duchamp.* Trans. Ron Padgett. New York: Viking Press, 1971.

Calinescu, Matei. *Five Faces of Modernity: Modernism, Avant-Garde, Decadence, Kitsch, Postmodernism.* Durham, NC: Duke University Press, 1987.

140 Carrouges, Michel. *André Breton and the Basic Concepts of Surrealism*. Trans. Maura
◇   Prendergast. Tuscaloosa: University of Alabama Press, 1974.

Castriota, David, ed. *Artistic Strategy and the Rhetoric of Power: Political Uses of Art from Antiquity to the Present*. Carbondale: Southern Illinois University Press, 1986.

Chipp, Herschel, ed. *Theories of Modern Art*. Berkeley: University of California Press, 1968.

Christo: The Umbrella Joint Project for Japan and USA. Press release. Oct. 9, 1991.

Collingwood, R. G. *The Principle of Art*. New York: Oxford University Press, 1958.

Costantino, Maria. *Frank Lloyd Wright*. New York: Crescent Books, 1991.

Coplans, John. *Andy Warhol*. New York: New York Graphic Society Ltd., 1969.

Croce, Benedetto. *Guide to Aesthetics*. Trans. Patrick Romanell. South Bend, IN: Regnery/Gateway, 1979.

Danto, Arthur C. *Embodied Meanings: Critical Essays and Aesthetic Meditations*. New York: Farrar, Straus and Giroux, 1994.

———. *The Transfiguration of the Commonplace: A Philosophy of Art*. Cambridge: Harvard University Press, 1981.

de Duve, Thierry. *Kant after Duchamp*. Cambridge: MIT Press, 1996.

Deitch, Jeffrey. "The New Economics of Environmental Art." In *Art in the Land: A Critical Anthology of Environmental Art*. Ed. Alan Sonfist. New York: E. P. Dutton, 1983.

Derrida, Jacques. *The Truth in Painting*. Chicago: University of Chicago Press, 1987.

Dewey, John. *Art as Experience*. New York: Capricorn Books, 1973.

D'Harnoncourt, Anne, and Kynaston McShine, eds. *Marcel Duchamp*. Exhibition catalog. New York: Museum of Modern Art, 1973.

Diamonstein, Barbaralee. *Inside the Art World: Conversations with Barbaralee Diamonstein*. New York: International Publications, 1994.

Eagleton, Terry. *The Ideology of the Aesthetic*. Cambridge: Basil Blackwell, 1990.

Eco, Umberto. *The Limits of Interpretation*. Indianapolis: Indiana University Press, 1990.

Fineberg, Jonathan. *Art since 1940: Strategies of Being*. Englewood Cliffs, NJ: Prentice Hall, 1995.

Fischer, Ernst. *The Necessity of Art: A Marxist Approach*. New York: Penguin Books, 1963.

Foucault, Michel. *The Order of Things: An Archaeology of the Human Sciences* [1966]. New York: Vintage Books, 1970.

Franscina, Francis. *Pollock and After: The Critical Debate*. New York: Harper & Row, 1985.

Friedman, Milton. *Capitalism and Freedom* [1962]. Chicago: University of Chicago Press, 1982.

Gidal, Peter. *Andy Warhol Film and Paintings: The Factory Years*. New York: Da Capo Press, 1987.

Gilbert, Rita. *Living with Art,* 4th ed. New York: McGraw Hill, 1995.

Goetzmann, William H., and William N. Goetzmann. *The West of the Imagination*. New York: W. W. Norton, 1986.

Goheen, Ellen R. *Christo: Wrapped Walk Ways*. New York: Harry N. Abrams, 1978.

Goldberg, Edward L. *After Vasari: History, Art and Patronage in Late Medici Florence*.

Princeton, NJ: Princeton University Press, 1988.

Gombrich, E. H. *Art and Illusion: A Study in the Psychology of Pictorial Representations*. Princeton, NJ: Princeton University Press, 1960.

Goodman, Nelson. *Languages of Art*. Indianapolis: Hackett Publishing, 1976.

———. *Ways of Worldmaking*. Indianapolis: Hackett Publishing, 1978.

Greenberg, Clement. "The Avant-Garde and Kitsch." In *Twentieth- Century Art Theory: Urbanism, Politics, and Mass Culture*. Edited by Richard Hertz and Norman M. Klein. Englewood Cliffs, NJ: Prentice Hall, 1990.

———. *The Collected Essays and Criticism*. Chicago: University of Chicago Press, 1988.

Groopman, Jerome. "Decoding Destiny," *New Yorker* (Feb. 9, 1998): 40–42.

Gruen, John. *Keith Haring: The Authorized Biography*. New York: Prentice Hall, 1991.

Hammacher, Abraham Marie. *René Magritte*. Trans. James Brockway. New York: H. N. Abrams, 1974.

Haring, Keith. *Keith Haring Journals*. New York: Viking, 1996.

Harrison, Charles, and Fred Orton, eds. *Modern Criticism: Alternate Contexts for Art*. New York: Harper & Row, 1984.

Hegel, G. W. F. *On Art, Religion, Philosophy: Introductory Lectures to the Realm of Absolute Spirit* [1831]. Ed. J. Glenn Gray. New York: Harper & Row, 1970.

Honnef, Klaus. *Andy Warhol, 1928–1987: Commerce into Art*. Cologne: Benedikt Taschen Verlag, 1990.

Hulten, K. G. Pontus. *The Machine as Seen at the End of the Mechanical Age*. New York: Museum of Modern Art, 1968.

Ionesco, Eugene. *Notes and Counter-Notes* [1962]. Trans. Donald Watson. London: J. Calder, 1964.

James, William. *The Varieties of Religious Experience* [1902]. New York: New American Library, 1958.

Jameson, Fredric. *Marxism and Form: Twentieth-Century Dialectical Theories of Literature*. Princeton, NJ: Princeton University Press, 1971.

Johnson, Brooks, and Thomas W. Styron. *Still Modern after All These Years*. Exhibition catalog. Norfolk, VA: Chrysler Museum, 1982.

Jones, Alan, and Laura de Coppet. *The Art Dealers*. New York: Clarkson N. Potter, 1984.

Judovitz, Dalia. *Unpacking Duchamp: Art in Transit*. Berkeley: University of California Press, 1998.

Kant, Immanuel. *The Critique of Judgement* [1790]. Oxford: Clarendon Press, 1964.

Klein, Ulrike. *The Business of Art Unveiled: New York Art Dealers Speak Up*. Frankfurt, Germany: Peter Lang, 1994.

Kornbluth, Jesse. *Pre-Pop Warhol*. New York: Random House, 1988.

Kramer, Hilton. *The Age of the Avant-Garde*. New York: Farrar Straus, 1973.

Kramer, Jane. *Whose Art Is It?* Durham, NC: Duke University Press, 1994.

Krauss, Rosalind E. *The Originality of the Avant-Garde and Other Modernist Myths*. Cambridge: MIT Press, 1985.

Kuh, Katherine. *The Open Eye*. New York: Harper & Row, 1971.

Kundera, Milan. *The Unbearable Lightness of Being*. Trans. Michael Henry Heim. New York: Harper & Row, 1984.

Kuspit, Donald. *The Cult of the Avant-Garde Artist*. Cambridge: Cambridge University Press, 1993.

142   Laporte, Dominique. *Christo* [1985]. Paris: Art Press/Flammarion, 1986.

◇   Léger, Fernand. "The Machine Aesthetic, the Manufactured Object, the Artisan and the Artist." In *Functions of Painting* [1965]. Ed. Edward F. Fry. Trans. Alexandra Anderson. New York: Viking Press, 1973.

Leppert, Richard. *Art and the Committed Eye: The Cultural Functions of Imagery.* Boulder, CO: Westview Press, 1996.

Lyotard, Jean-François. *Duchamp's Trans/formers* [1977]. Trans. Ian McLeod. Venice, CA: Lapis Press, 1990.

———. *The Inhuman: Reflections on Time* [1988]. Trans. Geoffrey Bennington and Rachel Bowlby. Stanford, CA: Stanford University Press, 1991.

———. *The Postmodern Condition: A Report on Knowledge* [1979]. Trans. Geoffrey Bennington and Brian Massumi. Minneapolis: University of Minnesota Press, 1984.

Machine Art. Exhibition catalog [1934]. New York: Museum of Modern Art, 1969.

Machlup, Fritz. *The Production and Distribution of Knowledge in the United States.* Princeton, NJ: Princeton University Press, 1962.

Mann, Paul. *The Theory-Death of the Avant-Garde.* Bloomington: Indiana University Press, 1991.

Marcuse, Herbert. *The Aesthetic Dimension: Toward the Critique of Marxist Aesthetics.* Toronto: Unitarian Universalist Association, 1977.

———. *One-Dimensional Man: Studies in the Ideology of Advanced Industrial Society.* Boston: Beacon Press, 1964.

McEvilley, Thomas. "Yves Klein, Messenger of the Age of Space," *Artforum* xx, no. 5 (1982):38–51.

McLuhan, Marshall. *Understanding Media: The Extension of Man.* Cambridge: MIT Press, 1994.

Meuris, Jacques. *René Magritte.* Trans. J. A. Underwood. Woodstock, NY: Overland Press, 1990.

Meyer, Ursula. *Conceptual Art.* New York: E. P. Dutton, 1972.

Nietzche, Friedrich. *Twilight of the Idols/The Anti-Christ.* Trans. R. J. Hollingdale. London: Penguin, 1968.

Noel, Bernard. *Magritte.* New York: Crown, 1976.

Nye, David E. *American Technological Sublime.* Cambridge: MIT Press, 1994.

O'Brien, Glenn. "Bop Art: Interview with Andy Warhol." *Artforum* xx, no. 6 (1982): 43–51.

O'Doherty, Brian. *Inside the White Cube: The Ideology of the Gallery Space.* San Francisco: Lapis Press, 1986.

Paley, Morton D. *Apocalyptic Sublime.* New Haven: Yale University Press, 1986.

Paz, Octavio. *Marcel Duchamp.* New York: Seaver Books, 1973.

Peterson, Elmer. *Tristan Tzara: Dada and Surrational Theorist.* New Brunswick, NJ: Rutgers University Press, 1971.

Poggioli, Renato. *The Theory of the Avant-Garde* [1962]. Trans. Gerald Fitzgerald. Cambridge: Harvard University Press, 1968.

Pound, Ezra. *Machine Art and Other Writings.* Durham, NC: Duke University Press, 1996.

Restany, Pierre. *Yves Klein*. New York: Harry N. Abrams, 1982.

Rubell, Jason. "Keith Haring: The Last Interview," *Arts Magazine* 65 (September 1990):52–59.

Rush, Richard H. *Art as an Investment*. Englewood Cliffs, NJ: Prentice Hall, 1961.

Sassower, Raphael. *Technoscientific Angst: Ethics + Responsibility*. Minneapolis: University of Minnesota Press, 1997.

Sayre, Henry M. *The Object of Performance: The American Avant-Garde since 1970*. Chicago: University of Chicago Press, 1989.

Schwartz, Arturo. *Marcel Duchamp*. Milan: Fabri, 1968.

Shattuck, Roger. *The Innocent Eye*. New York: Farrar, Straus and Giroux, 1985.

Senie, Harriet F. *Contemporary Public Sculpture: Tradition, Transformation, and Controversy*. New York: Oxford University Press, 1992.

Shlain, Leonard. *Art and Physics: Parallel Visions in Space, Time, and Light*. New York: William Morrow, 1991.

Simmel, Georg. *The Philosophy of Money* [1900]. Trans. Tom Bottomore and David Frisby. London: Routledge and Kegan Paul, 1978.

Snow, C. P. *The Two Cultures: And a Second Look* [1959]. Cambridge: Cambridge University Press, 1969.

Sonfist, Alan, ed. *Art in the Land: A Critical Anthology of Environmental Art*. New York: E. P. Dutton, 1983.

Spies, Werner. *Christo: The Running Fence Project*. New York: Harry N. Abrams, 1977.

Sporre, Dennis J. *The Creative Impulse*. Englewood Cliffs, NJ: Prentice Hall, 1987.

Steiner, Wendy. *The Scandal of Pleasure*. Chicago: University of Chicago Press, 1995.

Stephan, Paula, and Sharon Levin. *Striking the Mother Lode in Science: The Importance of Age, Place, and Time*. New York: Oxford University Press, 1992.

Stiles, Kristine, and Peter Selz, eds. *Theories and Documents of Contemporary Art: A Sourcebook of Artists' Writings*. Berkeley: University of California Press, 1996.

Sylvester, David. *Magritte*. New York: Praeger, 1969.

Thompson, Edward P. *William Morris: Romantic to Revolutionary* [1955]. Stanford, CA: Stanford University Press, 1976.

Tomkins, Calvin. *The Bride and the Bachelors: Five Masters of the Avant-Garde: Duchamp, Tinguely, Cage, Rauschenberg, Cunningham*. New York: Viking Press, 1965.

———. *The Scene: Reports on Post-Modern Art*. New York: Viking Press, 1976.

Vaughan, William. *Romanticism and Art*. New York: Thames and Hudson, 1994.

Wallace, David. "Unwrapping Christo," *Empire Magazine of the West* (Sept. 8, 1996):14–15, 18, 24.

Warhol, Andy. *America*. New York: Harper & Row, 1985.

———. *The Philosophy of Andy Warhol*. New York: Harcourt Brace Jovanovich, 1975.

Weisman, Steven R. "Christo's International Umbrella Project," *New York Times*, Nov. 13, 1990.

Weschler, Lawrence. "Value: I—A Fool's Questions," *New Yorker* (Jan. 18, 1988):33–56.

———. "Value: II—Category Confusion," *New Yorker* (Jan. 25, 1988):88–98.

Wheeler, Daniel. *Art since Mid-Century: 1945 to the Present*. Englewood Cliffs, NJ: Prentice Hall, 1991.

144 Wolff, Janet. *The Social Production of Art.* 2nd ed. New York: New York University
◇   Press, 1993.
     Yard, Sally. *Christo: Oceanfront.* Princeton, NJ: Art Museum, Princeton University,
         1975.
     Yves Klein 1928–1962: A Retrospective. Exhibition catalog. Houston, TX: Institute for
         the Arts, Rice University, 1982.

Index

Cultural Frames, Framing Culture

Books in this series examine both the way our culture frames our narratives and the way our narratives produce the culture that frames them. Attempting to bridge the gap between previously disparate disciplines, and combining theoretical issues with practical applications, this series invites a broad audience to read contemporary culture in a fresh and provocative way.

Nancy Martha West
Kodak and the Lens of Nostalgia

Raphael Sassower and Louis Cicotello
The Golden Avant-Garde:
Idolatry, Commercialism, and Art